Introverts

How Introverts Can Find Love and Have Better Relationships

(Practical Tools to Leverage Your Strengths and Expand Your Network)

Jared Cruz

Published By **Region Loviusher**

Jared Cruz

Introverts: How Introverts Can Find Love and Have Better Relationships (Practical Tools to Leverage Your Strengths and Expand Your Network)

ISBN   978-1-7774976-5-1

Legal & Disclaimer

Table Of Contents

Chapter 1: Recharging Your Batteries - Finding Solitude in an Extroverted World

The worldwide is mostly a noisy and noisy location, entire of stimulation and situations that constantly require us to react or respond. All this drains energy from an introvert, and they usually need greater time to recharge after each power expenditure. Even seemingly simple responsibilities like walking errands might also placed on us out. Let's have a have a look at a few suitable strategies to come out clean and geared up to take on the challenges of lifestyles in an extroverted global.

I Am Who I Am

Learning to surely accept who you're and what makes you tick is the crucial issue to surviving as an introvert in a international that encourages us to assignment a sure photograph. Don't try and be the existence of the celebration in case you're not. Don't question what you're comfortable with.

Embrace it and make your self satisfied doing what you want. You aren't supporting genuinely anybody, least of all your self, by means of way of the usage of pretending to be something which you aren't. Once you display that you are satisfied with how you're, others will recognize and recognize that.

It goes deeper than this, however. Ph.D., assistant psychology professor at Davis and Elkins College and writer of Introvert Power Laurie Helgoe says that introverts who forgo their right nature genuinely decentre themselves from their intuition. The further you get out of your actual country, the quicker you may burn out.

Let It Go

The beyond, that is. It's prolonged lengthy beyond and executed with, so there's no aspect in looking returned. You might probable look decrease back at your younger years and choice you had hung out with that cool company extra, or lengthy beyond to greater activities, however bear in mind that

that's now not what made you tick and you possibly wouldn't were comfortable doing those topics except.

The Best Policy

Honesty, this is. An introvert certainly wants to be honest with themselves and one-of-a-type people. Can I virtually deal with taking my determine's distant places friends on an afternoon-long tour of our town? Do I really need to spend four hours at my friend's birthday party? If the solution isn't any, decline gracefully. Expressing your barriers in truth to your self and people spherical you can assist you to be the first-class you will be.

Really take an honest check what you want to be happy and energised. Only even as you're fulfilled can you deliver your great and have first-rate relationships with others, be they circle of relatives or that particular someone.

The Big WHY

Always go lower back to the large WHY in the again of your each movement. When this is smooth for your head, you can skip ahead collectively together with your energies focussed for your motivation. You can reduce out the pointless with a purpose to drain your energy. The large why may additionally even power you along when the going gets hard.

Streamline

Once you're sincere with your self, you're capable of select out the humans, occasions, duties and locations that will be predisposed to suck your strength. Who do you no longer sense comfortable with? What obligations leave you feeling such as you need to recharge? Also emerge as aware about the matters that make you experience energized and terrific. You can then start to weed out the electricity-suckers from your life to make room for extra remarkable hobbies.

Where's The Ceiling?

Introverts aren't damaging to interaction, they just want to position a limit on it. Understand simply how a good deal stimulation you can take earlier than you begin to get uncomfortable, then call a time-out. Pay interest on your physical cues, Helgoe advises. "We apprehend at a cell degree even as we're dropping steam - we may moreover begin to experience stressed, bored, or maybe headachy."

Also apprehend that you want time to warmth as lots as a person or situation. Give it time, analyzing a person little by little. Be OK with vetoing an impromptu engagement which you weren't mentally prepared for.

My Space, My Time

Create your very own little glad area wherein you could recharge in peace. Decorate it and fill it with things that make you satisfied. Spend first-class time there unwinding and getting into a peaceful country doing the matters that you love, be it writing, drawing or perhaps dancing. Make satisfactory you block out time for this. Don't convey your telephone in with you, try to block out any outside distractions or even regulate the lighting in your consolation degree.

The Lightbulb

Take benefit of your by myself time, as it's at the same time as you're by myself which you get current. You will in all likelihood enjoy that your progressive juices start to drift during your downtime … make certain you harness them with the aid of way of maintaining a notepad or a few shape of recording device nearby. Aim to record a mean of 30 mind a day so that you don't lose the addiction. It's even more important to seize the ones flighty notions for the cause which you have got nobody else that will help you consider them or bounce them off.

Create New Worlds

Introverts generally don't unique themselves, who opt to hold their feelings and mind to themselves. It's well to locate an outlet to express your self creatively. If you love song, play an device or sing inside the direction of your 'me' time. If you unique your self through artwork, pursue that during your downtime. Write, if that evokes you, or pursue pix. Get out of area in a worldwide that you create for your self, and you may pop out refreshed.

Hobby Horse

Pick up a interest in which you could channel your power into a few component effective however calming. Something like strolling or trekking is first rate - you could get healthful and revel in your solitude at the same time. If others be part of you, you have got got got the excuse that you're too out of breath to speak!

Creative pastimes are also a first rate manner to channel your power and research new matters. If you're now not too keen on assembly new human beings and having to be part of a set, don't worry. The hobby itself is an excuse to sit quietly and consciousness your power on a few factor.

Push It

In accepting that you decide on matters to be predictable and at your very very own pace, it's additionally suitable to provide yourself a touch push every sometimes. Never get too comfortable interior your private limitations that they turn out to be walls. Seek out new and adventurous conditions on your private way and stretch your horizons. It can be a small detail like speakme to an sudden person in a social putting, or a large element like taking up volunteer art work, but the ones are the matters on the way to increase you into a larger person.

Keep Good Company

Seeing as how you're greater cushty with a small organization of circle of relatives and pals as a substitute of having many buddies, encircle your self with folks that faucet into the one of a kind sides of your persona and improve your life in exceptional strategies. They will achieve you for who you are, however on the same time mold and shape you through the usage of hard you indoors your consolation ranges.

Use your herbal inclination in the direction of depth to increase close to ties with those humans, a closeness and don't forget a good way to come up with a steady area from which to find out and venture out into the area.

Take a Break

A mini-retreat is critical to an introvert's nicely-being, so time table one in each from time to time. Spend one or 2 days far from the normal hustle and bustle of your existence; take a weekend away, if you could. Plan to do not anything lots within the course of that factor, absolutely wander or stress round taking within the points of interest and sounds spherical you.

If you may't escape from domestic, surely logging off social media for a couple of days looks as if a holiday. You may additionally artwork on the park to get some smooth air and a trade of surroundings. A lovely manner of breaking from habitual is relationship your self for the entire day. Have a picnic, then pass watch a film … inquisitive about your personal!

Take Care

Take care of me, myself and I. Exercise and consume properly. Get outside on every occasion you could and perform a little form of calming, centring interest like yoga, meditation or qigong.

Take care of others too. Volunteer in a few element you're captivated with, be it animals, orphans, catastrophe remedy or the aged. Spreading your love and abundance will remind you of the way valuable you're, and get you from your shell in a powerful way.

Self-Improvement

Constantly try to enhance yourself via take a look at, pushing boundaries or dealing with stressful conditions head-on. Avoid being too crucial, however behavior regular self-contemplated photo and surely be sincere about what you would like to look yourself doing better. It can also be a few issue tangible, like your English, or your cooking competencies.

Chapter 2

Having Meaningful Relationships

1. Kith and Kin

You love your own family; they may be your lifestyles, your love, your satisfaction. You dad and mom, youngsters and family - these human beings are to your lifestyles through thick or thin and you love them unconditionally. You may also supply a few thing you may to motive them to happy, and you recognize they might do the same for you. You must make their puzzle portions wholesome into yours, come what may additionally, however for an introvert, this isn't smooth.

The regular needs on you - your highbrow, religious and physical electricity will depart you tired in case you aren't careful. How do you create enormous, alluring relationships even as although searching after your introverted needs?

• Early Birds Catch the Worm

Wake up more early, regardless of the fact that it's terrific 15 minutes, to spend a while without a doubt free of any distractions or every person's desires. Do something to decorate your strength, be it yoga, a walk, or the first cup of espresso mostly on your very own. Try to clear your thoughts of some thing for that span of time which will virtually price up.

• Create Your Own Space

Carve out a touch oasis for yourself. Ideally this would be to your mattress room, but if now not, then discover a small alcove or the attic or basement. Fit it out with topics that make you satisfied and comfortable, and ensure you spend some time in it every day doing belongings you revel in.

If bodily area is surely now not viable, create internal region through blocking off out out of doors stimulation. Put on headphones and retreat into your tune. Just remember now not to get sincerely out of place for your private global.

• Get Out

Take any opportunity to step out for a few on my own time if you want it. Offer to run errands that need to be finished, or simply move for a stroll. Be lightly enterprise agency if a person asks to return along, telling them which you need the time on my own, but you'll be decrease back with them in real time.

• The 2 Letter Word

Sometimes, mainly in terms of family engagements, you honestly want to draw the road as to how a tremendous deal you can control in advance than you need to detach and collect your electricity. Don't be afraid to say, 'no' and observe it up through explaining why you could't do a little aspect at that second. It's amazing to unique your desires while you're no longer frazzled, so do it early whilst your strength hasn't run out. It's additionally appropriate to give an explanation for that your requests for on my own time are actually critical so that you will be your outstanding self.

• Share and Care

Whatever you do to guard your inner area, bear in thoughts that those are human beings whom you like and who love you. They will admire your need for area, but their want to percentage to your existence and strength is crucial too, so preserve in mind to offer reassurances which you're no longer deliberately pushing them away, you sincerely need the time to recharge so that you'll be there for them to your complete ability.

• Flexibility is Key

In keeping with sharing and being involved, recollect to be flexible. You may not usually be capable of have all the time or region you need to completely recharge, but make the fantastic of the time you have got and channel some component strength you have got were given into the people you like.

~The Best Job in the World~

Parenting is a whole-time job which you get precious few breaks from, particularly in case your children are nonetheless greater younger. Even night time time time time can be taken over, no longer to mention bathroom time, quiet time, artwork time … You are required to be there for psychical assistance, further to intellectual and emotional manual. Your entire being is on name for pretty an awful lot 24 hours.

Introverted parents are made to revel in that they may be lots much less than what they must be. They revel in that they should have fun with their every 2d with their youngsters and when they don't they experience inadequate and, worse, responsible. Accept that you can pleasant be your splendid self, even for your children, when you have had time to device, recharge, and renew yourself.

1. Drop the Guilt

Feeling responsible is counter-effective and satisfactory drains your valuable electricity. Just take delivery of the way you are stressed out and artwork with it. Introversion or extroversion is without a doubt how we're stressed, regardless of the whole thing, an real natural worried placing that we

can't alternate, but only mild.

2. Compromise

If you're capable of, tweak areas of your lifestyles to lessen your energy-drain. Cut down on social interactions at artwork, or do matters remotely, like deliver emails as an alternative of having meetings. Also have a look at your social commitments. You can simplest unfold your self so thinly, and your precedence needs to be your youngsters.

3. Their Time, My Time

If you work from home, you may although be invested on your children's goings-on, even if you have Mary Poppins as your nanny. The fine element for each you and your kids might be to send them to day-care or nursery wherein they're able to carve out their non-public international away from you. You can then definitely have your non-public time and location.

four. Quiet Time

Family quiet time is important to keep topics jogging easily

in a circle of relatives. Half an hour of analyzing or quiet play in your youngsters lets in you realign and moreover teaches your children to understand quiet play. Bear in thoughts that your infant may additionally moreover want those treasured recharge moments.

~Handling the Holidays~

Holidays are particularly draining for introverts. Relatives and pals all need to see you, you're anticipated to wait all types of social gatherings and, when you have children, they will be domestic and expecting leisure. Your youngsters's grandparents might also additionally anticipate to spend some superb time with them, too.

1. Free Babysitting!

Take benefit of the truth that your mother and father need to spend time along aspect your kids ... use them as babysitters! Drop them off for a day of amusing and revel in yourself - introvert style! Recharge, and renew yourself. This is going for any accomplice and youngsters who're willing, too.

2. Care-pool

Don't neglect approximately that other dad and mom may additionally even want their by myself time, so recommend care-pooling. Take turns to host play dates and organise sports to hold them occupied. They can bake cookies, make decorations, or maybe watch a movie, and the adults could have their own little gathering or go do what they need to do.

3. Bring Them Along

Do you understand that you have a right away buddy to carry to the myriad of social vacation gatherings? Children will deflect the focal point off you, offer you with a speakme component, and, at the same time as worse includes worse, you have got got an excuse to no longer talk to others ... you're tending for your toddler! You moreover have an smooth escape plan even as your infant receives careworn.

4. I Need My Space

If you want to tour domestic for the holidays, probabilities are that you'll be anticipated to stay at your parents' or family' houses. This is probably worrying for an introvert - you normally don't have any vicinity for your self, and you're continuously anticipated to smile, be engaged and gift at each meal desk. Politely insist that you'll live at a lodge in which you may have a few privateness and peace. If your own family surely

insists you live with them, compromise via the usage of staying for a few nights after which retiring to a hotel. You can lessen the emotional guilt via the usage of manner of saying that you want your children to experience something extraordinary, probable.

five. Cut It Short

Arrange to arrive at a family amassing close to mealtime so you obtained't should drain your power with long hours of interaction earlier. If you're staying over, get lower decrease lower back on your very own location an afternoon earlier, if you may. You'll then have a day to get nicely and regroup earlier than heading back in to paintings day after today. Even look at decreasing your adventure time shorter, if feasible, with the aid of using using taking a plane or educate in preference to using. Being out and about way you can't truly recharge in peace.

6. Be a Taskmaster

Prepare jobs for own family coming to live with you simply so they'll be occupied and plenty much less likely to take in a while. Ask the sister who loves to prepare dinner to help with the food training. The available brother can assist your husband repair topics round

the residence. The children can get busy adorning the region. An introduced bonus is that introverted website site visitors additionally may be placed at ease with some thing to do.

2. The Love of Your Life

Relationships are lovely, but not smooth to navigate for any type of character. There is generally the stress of setting up up and exposing our vulnerability, satisfactory to be left massive open and on my own. There is likewise the priority of the opportunity - the danger of becoming out of place in someone

21

else, of being engulfed of their lifestyles, want and dreams.

The introvert has it even extra tough - we fear every being engulfed and deserted on the identical time. We need to figure out the manner to allow people in, but at the equal time, we are scared that they received't love our real self and that they may push us away. We need to work doubly hard to keep our non-public little vicinity whilst setting up it up simply enough to allow a person else in.

• Deep Analysis

Look for the triggers that drain your strength. What conditions zap you? Analyse the times you revel in you want quiet. What perks you up at the ones low moments? Also check which conditions take you an prolonged time to get over.

Pay hobby to whether or not or not you have periods at some point of which your energy levels are better or lower in giant. Does it take a look at the seasons or the times of the week? All this allows you to pinpoint even as and the way you may be at your splendid together together with your companion, and while you want to be by myself.

It is likewise crucial to test how prolonged you need to relax out after an hassle. You can then step some distance from the state of affairs with a clean idea of while you could come once more to it to remedy problems.

• PDAs ... Yes or No?

Gary Chapman recommend a contemporary concept within the five Love Languages that lets in us apprehend the methods wherein we maximum simply provide and take love:

-        Quality Time - time spent collectively doing fun and good sized matters.

-        Physical Touch - Physical expressions of love and affection.

-        Gifts - Presents, massive or small trinkets.

-     Words of Affirmation - verbal expressions of love, encouragement and acknowledgement.

-     Acts of Service - topics carried out in your partner that brighten their life and vice versa.

None of these are proper or wrong, it's definitely how we're cushty expressing our emotions. Accept and artwork with this, allow your companion understand, and moreover recognize how they unique themselves too, so that you realise what works tremendous for each of you.

• Communication ... It Works!

You need to talk your want and desires. Nobody knows your inner speak except you and it's as an entire lot as you to inform your companion while you need to be left on my own to recharge or art work through some thing on your head. Even in a demanding scenario - as an instance after an argument, clean communique as to how an entire lot time you want to determine things out for your head will pass a long way toward diffusing matters.

Be particular while you talk your wishes. This is to reassure your associate that you genuinely do need to be on my own, or that you want sparkling air. You may be able to workout session how each of you could get what you need - if your associate desires to get to realise his boss better but you don't feel up to getting all dressed up and going to a eating place, you could suggest they come over for dinner.

This is going for a way you offer and get hold of affection too. Once you've determined the way you and your companion most quite truly express and obtain love, have an open communicate approximately it. You will then each be more receptive and appreciative of the other's love expressions, which in flip will inspire them to give more of them.

• What Are Your Boundaries

Nothing is black and white, and no longer the whole lot is draining to an introvert. Find out what conditions are extra bearable or unbearable for you and why. Maybe you don't like going to occasions in which you don't apprehend every body, but if it have turn out to be a assembly of near pals it might be OK. Negotiate inner your barriers, and you may discover a center floor.

• Time Is Precious

Quality time - each couple desires it. Figure out the manner you best need to spend it and speak that together collectively along with your accomplice. To him, top notch time might probably imply partying together, on the equal time as you'll be happy simply snuggling in mattress and studying. Once he's aware of what could make you happy, you each can revel in some component collectively.

• New Friends

If you're dating an extrovert, they may likely have a big institution of buddies and they'll possibly want to loaf around with them. You might not experience snug in the ones conditions, but due to the reality that your associate is buddies with them, it's unfair to prevent them, and in addition unfair to strain your self to loaf around with them.

Try to exit as a pair and meet new buddies with whom you every have some thing in commonplace. Attend sports activities you every experience and make like-minded pals.

• Compromise… A Many Splendored Thing

They say compromise is the essential component to any relationship, and that is actual to an extent. Remember that compromise is a -manner street. It might be the each of you doing some thing which you're each cushty with. It could be the 2 of you doing what your partner desires to do that time, after which what they want to do next time. Or which you every do your very own matters at some degree. Just make sure which you are every aware of and agreeable to the compromise.

• Check In

You've controlled to steer your partner to do something calm and quiet with you. Keep in mind, even though, that it's no longer something that they may generally pick out to entertain themselves with. Keep checking in on them every every now and then to make sure they may be nevertheless OK. Keep up a ordinary float of verbal exchange and your partner will admire it.

~The Dating Scene~

Dating … the word makes the maximum powerful man quiver, an lousy lot a good buy much less the internal-international loving introvert. Put myself available? Make idle chitchat with a person I don't recognize? Pretend to be into each little element they do to try and provoke me? Subject myself to severe, non-public questions?? No thanks! Take coronary heart with those pointers on a manner to stay on a date … and in all likelihood locate love! Or at least have a superb time.

1. What Works For You

Only you will apprehend what works for you, so interest on what you need and align your energy to have that display up. If 'setting your self available' honestly obtained't give you the results you want, don't do it. If you're snug gaining knowledge of a person on line, do it for so long as you want to.

2. Profiling

If you're making plans on installing area an online dating profile, throw in diffused guidelines approximately your introversion. Write approximately

things like your idea of a terrific date is a quiet, candle-lit dinner, or that your selected interest is curling up with a splendid e-book.

three. Buddies Breed Buddies

Get to realize new human beings thru your friends. That way, you realize that they'll be at the least of a similar mind-set and also you don't need to start from scratch socially with them. You may also have a talking-aspect for your introducer (discussing their well factors, with a piece of success!)

four. Remember Your Boundaries

Even if you're unexpectedly Ms or Mr Popularity, don't go date-crazy and line them up for each night of the week. You KNOW that you'll be an exhausted ruin via the quit of the week and that it's going to take a long time to get nicely.

Also recollect that in case you need to cancel due to the reality you sincerely don't revel in as an lousy lot as it, then cancel. There's no thing taking area a date in case your electricity is low … you won't have a splendid time

and nor will your date. Offer your date an trade get-collectively, and be specific approximately it simply so they acquired't feel you're blowing them off.

five. Set the Scene

If you place the scene through suggesting what to do or wherein to go for a date, you'll make sure which you'll as a minimum be comfortable in familiar environment, doing assets you enjoy and are assured doing and taking element in food which you understand and love. With the load of chartering surprising territory out of the manner, you could focus your power on studying your date.

6. Coach, Coach

Give your self a pep talk before a date, encouraging your self and on foot via any eventuality you might imagine of. Envision what you'll do and the way you'll react in every at once. You will then be extra organized and less flustered.

7. Instant Chemistry?

Connecting with a person isn't smooth for without a doubt all and sundry, and we already apprehend that that is what introverts find out hassle with. Don't assume your first actual stumble upon to be the exquisite spark-flying dream of rom-coms. Go in without a expectancies and you could have a remarkable time simply … having a first-rate time.

8. Where's My Wingman?

Do you sense the pressure of 1-on-one relationship is too much? Double date! Grab an extroverted buddy to be your wingman. They will ease you into the go together with the go with the flow of factors and smooth over any awkwardness. They can help maintain the verbal exchange (and wine) flowing, and you will likely have a better time of it.

nine. Front and Centre

Be honest about your introversion together with your associate for the night time time.

This will lessen any risk that they'll mistakenly see you as standoffish or bored to death.

10. Reframe

If you're annoying approximately whether or not or not your date will at the side of you reframe the query: are YOU inquisitive about THEM, not the opposite way round. Looking at it this way takes the threshold off it for you - you're no longer there to impress them, you're just there to have fun and get to understand someone.

eleven. Question Mark

Ask questions about your date that lets in you to encourage them to open up approximately themselves. Think of a few quirky or appealing questions which is probably certain to have you ever every laughing or chatting away - some thing alongside the lines of, "Which well-known individual you'll maximum like to satisfy?" or, "If you can pick, what animal could probably you want to be and why?"

12. Flip It Back

When you're asked a question, return the favour! After you've got answered, ask your date the identical questions. This will cause them to experience desired and moreover assist you increase the verbal exchange a chunk bit.

Be careful the manner you try this, despite the truth that. It has to experience herbal, otherwise it may bring about awkward moments.

3. Best Buddies

Society seems to count on that having a big range of pals and a whole calendar of social sports activities manner you're satisfied and fulfilled. This can be authentic for an extrovert, but the real contrary is actual for the introvert. Introverts are on the lookout for extraordinary over quantity. They don't want that multitude of friends, however of the few pals they do have, they trying to find depth.

Introverts approach friendship in any other way, often tending to anticipate that their buddies don't want constant input similar to them. It's vital to keep relationships, but, due to the truth the vintage adage of 'out of sight, out of mind' does preserve genuine. You can't actually be a lone ranger; you want a guide organization and circle of people with whom you will be truely yourself with. It's additionally important to make new connections so you boom as a person.

Keeping In Touch

• Ebb And Flow

Do realise and get hold of that there will normally be a few top day-and-bye buddies in your life, and there might be your real buddies for whom you can do a little factor and vice versa. Also understand that once in a while, within the go with the glide of lifestyles, close to friends may additionally additionally moreover come to be far off friends. Don't enjoy accountable about it. If you need to re-ignite the friendship, all once more, in reality do it. Take small steps to re-plug into their life.

• Pick Up the Phone

Keeping up on the side of your pals, or even your family, will usually include a aware attempt for an introvert. As in some thing, small steps toward your purpose assist to reduce the seemingly insurmountable mountain of calls, texts, gatherings and meet-ups. If you actually need to preserve your friendship with someone, virtually do it! Send a quick WhatsApp, email, Facebook poke, something to remind them that you're nevertheless in their universe. Schedule time to satisfy and re-join.

• Upon Reconnecting

Don't proportion all the reasons why you haven't been preserving in touch, nor must you sense you need to provide you with reasons. Just be honest and direct, provide a easy apology and provide to attempt to do higher any more. If the friendship have become sturdy within the starting, they may recognize. If they don't understand, you need to consider that perhaps the relationship wasn't so strong to begin with.

• Beware The Screen

While manifestly social media is an introvert's manner to preserving in contact, be cautious. The casual 'friending', liking or observation each every now and then clearly isolates your in addition from the real connection a friendship dreams.

We truly located forth a totally distorted picture of our lives on social media. Things are continuously out of context - you could submit, "I'm feeling down," and all your Facebook buddies would likely ship their properly-dreams but have no concept as to why.

Conversely, a 'girl's night time out' image can also provide you with the have an impact on that a today's friend is a celebration animal, a great manner to deter you from deepening the relationship because of the truth you revel in you acquired't have masses in not unusual with them, on the same time as in truth it changed into in fact a one-off event for his or her cousin's bridal ceremony.

New Connections

• Friendship Bonus

If you pursue an hobby due to the fact you actually discover it irresistible and are obsessed on it, you will meet like-minded humans. These are the human beings with whom you is probably possibly to shape lasting bonds with. This works because due to the fact you spend quite a while pursuing this hobby, you will be round the ones people pretty a honest bit. This will boom your opportunities of reading them and connecting with them. You will actually have a shared passion over which to bond with.

If you appear to enjoy sports activities sports in that you're predominantly by myself, strive pursuing them from a remarkable thoughts-set. If you revel in meditation, find out a meditation institution. Yoga training are super to investigate new poses at. And also connect with like-minded people.

• Awkwardness - A Given

Awkwardness isn't always unusual at maximum first meetings, in particular for introverts. Don't withstand this, virtually go along with the waft and even as you surpass this hiccup, subjects will flow extra or much less without difficulty. Resist the temptation to retreat again into your very very personal worldwide without a doubt due to the fact the small communicate isn't flowing.

• Can You Reach It?

Go for possible dreams with regards to making friends. Don't anticipate to discover your BFF virtually due to the fact you joined a new painting magnificence ... these things have a modicum of danger and take time. As lengthy as you're making little efforts inside the route of creating it take region, you may at the least open up possibilities.

Aim to hit a few feasible dreams at every occasion you attend. They may be setting up a verbal exchange with one or new faces, warmly greeting 4 acquainted faces, or mission small talk for at least five minutes.

Small Talk - How, Why, What For!?

Small communicate - the bane of an introvert's lifestyles. More often than now not, it's now not that introverts do no longer need to engage, it's extra that they choose a deeper degree of connection and a extra substantial interaction. Small speak, to them, isn't an great use in their precious electricity.

If you turn it around, but, you may discover that small talk is surely something that an introvert can excel in and revel in. You can take manage of the verbal exchange and steer it toward something great. Then you may get in, make your mark, and get out at the equal time due to the fact the going is good - keep in mind that first-rate is more critical than quantity.

You are probably now not self-indulgent in conversations, so that you genuinely make your communique partner feel that they'll be critical with the useful resource of absolutely tuning in to what they are announcing. This may be very favored in a international in which many human beings don't sincerely listen. Nurture this sense of priority with the aid of way of asking them questions about themselves - even some issue as everyday

as, "Have you think (insert new movie call right right here). What did you agree with you studied of it?" This is likewise an outstanding manner of now not having to contribute as a good buy to the communique - simply allow them to share.

As an introvert, you're probable greater intuitive. You can faucet into the emotions and hobbies of these you are speaking to, and use the ones as cues as to which manner to guide, or allow the communique to go along with the glide. Your hobby of your personal sensitivities additionally gives you empathy for distinct's feelings, so you recognize while to exchange course or gently pass deeper into a topic.

Small communicate can also moreover turn to trendy topics like contemporary activities. Make sure you've got got pre-prepared some speakme points approximately what's going on in the international so you can make contributions to those discussions, or use them to keep a conversation going.

Chapter 3

Mastering College

College is an extrovert's dream. You're continuously surrounded with the useful resource of human beings, noise and hobby. You're referred to as on to attend mixers, conferences, golf equipment, and lectures, and you cope with have a take a look at businesses, discussions and teenager drama. While that is fantastic for folks who can cope with it, it's a nightmare for introverts who want time and place to method topics. Avoid burnout thru being clever so you can revel in what they call the awesome time of your life.

Not a Burden

Remind yourself, introversion is OK! It's now not a stone round your neck, it's surely no longer. You just want to discover ways to manage it amidst the excitement of university and if you can, you'll have a blast like they are pronouncing you'll ... sincerely on your private manner.

Where to Go?

In the search for a college that fits your introverted nature, don't forget faculties that offer the opportunity for hundreds particular socializing styles. Look for people with many severa golf equipment and further-curricular sports that target each academic and social issues. Go for faculties that don't find out themselves with any precise exercise or pursuit, like sports activities sports or journalism.

While it looks as if a small university is the way to move, they do will be inclined to be very insular … every body knows everybody else and there are quite simple cliques. Larger universities are less tough to wander off in. They additionally have a tendency to have greater activity alternatives from which you may select out.

Additionally, robust sororities and fraternities provide a feel of network, constant with a college administrator. "Introverts who joined sororities did so exactly for the motive that the ones offer a direct community for people who don't choice to spend hundreds of time constructing masses of friendships, because that can be tough."

Physically, does the university experience like a place wherein introverts can be cushty? Are there quiet, calm places wherein you can have interaction in meditation or yoga? Are there natural oases like ponds, gardens and parks? Are the libraries set up with personal have a take a look at spaces? Does the university designate a few dorms to be "quiet zones" wherein partying isn't always allowed after unique times?

Keep Close

For your private sanity, undergo in mind finding a university near your area of basis. Natalie Friedman, NYU Assistant Dean of Students and Director of Learning, Teaching, and Research, Dean of Studies and Senior Class Dean at Barnard, and member of the Vassar English department says, "I see masses of university students who pass the united states to be at a school they expect is "appropriate" due to reputation or area (or because of the reality their dad and mom or grandparents went there, however they can be lots happier, given their temperaments, being within the path of domestic.

I knew a student from the west coast [of the States] who came east for faculty because her mom and grandmother attended the university she turned into attending. But she become a traditional introvert, and moreover a toddler who modified into touchy, very near her mom and siblings, and not very adventurous. She struggled with homesickness, which in flip led her to stay in her room masses and avoid social interplay with new human beings. As a forestall end end result, she didn't experience university as an awful lot as her mother did, which pressured her mom. In the cease, the pupil determined to switch to a school toward home, and whilst she made the choice, you may see the comfort on her face."

Seek Out The Like

When you are deciding on a subject of test, go through in thoughts occupations which might be appropriate for introverts' sensibilities. Those which can be more internally processed or don't actually incorporate people will fit your needs. You will then enjoy some time analyzing in relative solitude. Alternatively, select some electives in the ones fields.

A Haven to Hide In

Living in unsuitable dorms can be the bane of an introvert's college lifestyles. Sharing a place that is supposed to be private is a nightmare without a privacy the least bit, and a regular barrage of stimulation - your roommates snoring, their typing, the rustle of paper, the whispered conversations ... it'll all put on you down. Colleges that provide person rooms are the higher bet, or better but, your personal digs.

First and maximum critical, your dorm room need to be your haven, with a piece of luck yours and yours on my own. Try to installation grasp outs at unique pals' places or at cafes or the like. That way, you could continuously retreat in your room for the solitude you need.

Alone, Not Alone

Bear in thoughts that it's not wholesome hiding away in your room all the time, you acquired't expand as someone. Make it a element to get out, however spend it by myself if you need to. Have a meal or walk across the lovely campus or on the park thru yourself every sometimes and also you'll be recharged and refreshed for the following basketball recreation or observe organization.

Just Do It

It may additionally sound like a contradiction while you're being advised to be real to your desires and take time for yourself, but you do want to push your self to get to be had once in a while. Insist on attending carrying activities, visit parties and be part of golf equipment for subjects that interest you. College is a time to discover, and if you are smart about it, you'll get the tremendous out of a terrific revel in.

Timing Is Everything

Keeping your sanity amidst the hustle and bustle of campus lifestyles takes a few strategizing. Arrange to have as masses of your instructions as feasible early inside the morning, or overdue in the night time. You will then be transferring about campus in the direction of off-height hours at the same time as there's lots less taking vicinity, and you could experience the experience of stillness inside the environment.

The same is going for mealtimes, which might be typically chaotic, noisy and grating on an introvert's nerves. Try eating a bit in advance or later than the primary crowd and also you might be capable of capture some moments of treasured solitude.

Nooks and Crannies

The obvious place to look for peace and solitude would be the library, but, as you will be aware, libraries can turn out to be social hotbeds. Explore your campus library and you could find out its "silent spots" in which you may camp out.

Venture throughout the campus and also you'll discover secluded havens to cover in in your treasured on my own time. Look for homes and regions which can be hardly ever visited and also you'll find out cherished spaces of solitude amidst the beehive of interest. Take your paintings or a e-book there, or perhaps lunch. Be careful, although, and usually maintain safety in mind.

Some campus houses do feature balconies on a number of their flooring. These are often deserted, in order that they offer the correct hidey-hollow as a way to squirrel away in. Again, safety ought to be first, 2nd and 1/three.

Green, Green Everywhere

Most campuses are exceptionally dotted with spots of green all round. Ovals or gardens are obviously … herbal and you frequently feel peaceful at the identical time as surrounded through way of nature. The innate sense of expansiveness inspires peace and quiet, making them the proper region to 'cowl'.

Avoid At All Costs

Some places and instances of day on campus are truely introvert tension triggers, so keep away from them as despite the fact that your life trusted it. Lunchtime, at the same time as every Tom, Dick and Harry are rushing to be fed and to fulfill up with their pals, is an introvert no-pass. Places like pubs and cafeterias are intended for meeting up and giant boisterousness.

It seems that the homes that residence first-rate fields of study like employer or engineering have a propensity to be accumulating elements for social hobby, so steer clean of them if you're no longer inside the mood.

An interesting sociological phenomenon is that at most purposed gatherings, seating is prepared in a semi-circle format, or people are referred to as upon to shape a semi-circle. Similarly, groups are attracted to the semi-spherical arrangement. Avoid places wherein seating is arranged in this layout - they will draw crowds. Even appearance out for this form in architectural designs ... consider the Roman Coliseum?

The Unavoidable

You're round a number of humans transferring here and there ... accidental interplay is unavoidable. What do you do in the lecture hall, as an example? Head instantly for the yet again or the rims of the hall in order that you will be flanked with the aid of using the wall. From those vantage factors, you with out issues watch the courtroom cases with much less risk of being called upon.

Want to dissuade verbal exchange? Act busy and those will usually go away you by myself. Another way to save you small talk in its tracks? Show your now not-so-approachable face, but you want to glaringly use this tactic with caution.

Make your top notch try and avoid it, but in the end, you may't genuinely be a rock or an island ala Simon and Garfunkel, so every time you do come upon a state of affairs, cope with it, and then retreat as gracefully as viable.

Gather Your Gang

When you first arrive on campus, take some time to find out a few like-minded people with whom you sense comfortable. Just start speakme to whoever is round you - inside the lecture corridor, in the dorm, or sitting next to you within the cafeteria. Slowly growth a friendship with those people you click on with. A few excellent buddies are all you need, not a huge circle of pals.

Innies and Outties

Being among like-minded humans technique you may loosen up and be your self without questions and judgement. When you need some quiet time but don't need to be by myself, you could count on your innie buddies to hang around with you with out engaging or interacting in a way at the manner to empty you.

Don't depend the outties out, but. They may be your closest pals too, when they apprehend and appreciate in which you're coming from. They can bring you from your shell, which you want to do once in a while, to keep matters balanced.

Homies

It's no longer that you don't care as an awful lot for them anymore, it's simply which you aren't very good at reaching out to people, especially if you have to make the greater attempt of calling or emailing. Keep up your ties together along side your own family and friends back home, despite the fact that. These are the human beings who've recognized and cherished you for your complete existence to date, and they will constantly be there if you want to retreat to whilst you absolutely need to BE. No questions requested.

Express Yourself

If you're not geared up to speak up on your observe group or lecture, but you revel in you have were given some trouble to make contributions, request for some time together collectively along with your professor at their workplace. You can also electronic mail them. Remember that what you have got had been given to mention is treasured and well nicely well worth expressing, you simply ought to discover the proper second which you're cushty with.

DIY

Knitting calms you and gives you a feel of pleasure? DO it! You don't need to conform with distinct humans's idea of a laugh ... discover some element that turns your intellect or creativity on and pursue it. Don't worry if it appears nerdy to others; if you enjoy it, that's all that topics.

~Teaming Up~

We sometimes forget about about that kids moreover have their very very very own man or woman tendencies, but haven't discovered out to cope with them. Help your little one to stay sane inside the busy, busy international of school and play-dates wherein a number of their time entails being in a set.

1. Charge Up

Little introverts really need extra downtime to method the noisy worldwide. It's doubly vital for them because of the fact they don't even however have a whole records of 1/2 of of of what's taking place round them, and the way they should deal with it. Remind them to step away from the state of affairs each on occasion - a toilet damage or some outdoor time will perk them right up.

2. The Best Fit

Tell your infant to remember what he or she feels snug doing and what they experience they'll be accurate at.

Advise them to discover a feature doing what they may be snug doing, which for an introvert is commonly a within the decrease back of-the-scenes one.

Most introverts do nicely at solving problems due to the reality they make the effort to observe. They will see obligations via, so follow-up roles in shape them, as do element-oriented obligations. Creative duties moreover artwork for introverts.

3. One by way of One

An introvert is normally snug focusing on one element at a time - be it a assignment or speaking to humans. If your little one has thoughts to contribute to a group communicate but doesn't need to carry it as a outstanding deal because the complete organization, tell them to deliver it as a great deal as just one or of their teammates and permit them to help percentage it with the entire group.

Chapter four

Navigating the Social Scene

Socialising is unavoidable, you'll be referred to as upon to attend weddings and activities, cross clubbing, and so on and so forth. Small, intimate gatherings in which you already realize and are comfortable with maximum humans are what you're happiest with, however how do you navigate the ones massive bashes in that you don't recognize many people, the noise levels are excessive and the stimulation must get overwhelming?

Be a Night Owl

Night-time is generally while introverts want to be with the useful resource of the usage of themselves to lighten up and unwind, but it's truly the notable time to get out and mingle. This is because of the reality we are an awful lot less pressured at night time because of our cortisol tiers being at their lowest. When the cortisol tiers are low, you're more snug and you could deal with social situations with a greater degree head.

A (Wo) man with a Plan

Formulate a plan earlier than attending an occasion. Work out the way you want to play the scene - even all the way down to small information like in which you may feel greater comfortable fame or sitting, or who you need to purpose to comprehend with, if you apprehend the ones facts. Figure out at the same time as you need to leave. Even rehearse a hint if that permits to ease your anxiety.

The Plan Went Out the Window

For all of the improve planning you do, however, typically hold in mind that subjects will exchange. People who are alleged to be there might not be, you will possibly grow to be seated at some distinctive table, or the birthday celebration may end up moving to some other venue. Anticipate trade and you will be more likely to go together with the flow.

Tune In, Head Out

Jennifer B. Kahnweiler, PhD and creator of The Genius of Opposites, suggests spending some time plugging into yourself earlier than coming into a social setting. You can do some element proactive like meditate or repeat mantras or absolutely sit down down quietly for a while. Listening to calm song additionally works to calm the mind. Close your eyes, take sluggish, deep breaths and preserve but for a while.

The exceptional time to do this is certainly in advance than hitting the birthday celebration - to your automobile or on a bench outside. 10 to 15 minutes ought to be enough to fee you up.

Hit the Caffeine

According to Cain, coffee or some kind of caffeinated drink boosts your self assurance, electricity and positivity. She touts, "Coffee will deliver you from self-doubt. It gets you obsessed on new thoughts and permits you neglect about the refrain of judgers indoors your head. It propels your thinking and permits you're making connections among seemingly unrelated matters. Hence, the saying that 'a mathematician is a tool for turning coffee into theorems.' "

Have a cup of espresso or some particular caffeinated drink about half of of of an hour earlier than going to an event. Coffee takes approximately forty five mins to be absorbed into your gadget, and lasts round four to six hours, so have every other hit of caffeine spherical 2 hours into the event in case you anticipate you may be known as upon to stay for longer than 4 hours.

Bring a Friend

An extroverted friend, that is. Chances are, masses of your friends are extroverts, due to the fact that opposites enchantment to to stability each excellent out. Your extroverted friend may be your key to consolation in a get collectively, specifically in case you don't realize many human beings there. Helgoe says, "They'll understand you can not want to speak to truely all and sundry and might assist introduce you to people you'd like to connect to."

Your extroverted friend also can help to speak you up, and, even as the time comes, will apprehend your day out cues. They can then let you barter your social limits easily.

Hey Buddy!

Act like everyone is already your friend, even if you're actually meeting them for the number one time. Greet them warmly, ask about their paintings or own family, or enquire approximately existence in big. Don't forget to percentage approximately your self too!

Team Up

If you aren't capable of deliver a chum to an event, go searching the room for distinct introverts who appear to want help becoming a member of in. You might be greater snug talking to them because of the reality that they may possibly understand your awkwardness and understand your want for communique gaps. Team up and take turns putting in place conversations with others, lessening your danger of social burnout.

Stand Tall

Fake it 'til you are making it, touts John Zelenski, Ph.D., psychology partner professor at Carlton University. If you typically experience small, stand tall. If you're worrying about voicing out your opinion, voice it out louder. If you avoid interplay, make conscious eye touch. Keep being the man or woman you need to be via doing what they might do until you believe which you are that person.

Confident poses like straightening your spine, spreading your legs and putting your palms to your hips actually growth your cortisol and testosterone ranges, which enhances yourself perception, steady with social psychologist Amy Cuddy.

Laughter is the Best

You can be residing for your internal global, however you may reassure others round you which you aren't standoffish by means of using presenting a easy smile or direct eye contact.

A smile is visible as an extroverted trait. It makes us seem greater upbeat, social and approachable. Charles Darwin himself examined the technology of smiling in his e book The Expression of the Emotions in Man and Animals. It's no longer understood why, however the smooth smile sparks off bodily and emotional positivity in each the giver and the receiver, giving an without delay immoderate. Use its silent energy in your benefit. "A smile is the shortest distance among humans," regular with entertainer Victor Borge.

A real snigger whilst some thing humorous arises suggests that notwithstanding the fact which you're now not a clown through nature, you do however understand humour and which you are … human.

Get Out of Your Head

Introverts are typically happier assignment their very private inner speak than undertaking idle chit-chat with others, however in order to be truly happy, you cannot cowl away to your non-public head all of the time. You ought to discover a comfortable stability amongst retaining your very own area and interacting with the out of doors international. In a social setting, make a conscious effort to get from your head for a bit at the same time as and keep conversations you can typically reduce quick. If you don't need to contribute an excessive amount of, you can use your listening capabilities to inspire the alternative person to talk extra. You may also moreover look at or gain a few thing in the method.

One Mouth, Two Ears

You recognize the well-known announcing ... we're all given one mouth and ears, so use them as a result. Introverts are clearly better listeners. We aren't impatient to push our component and we without a doubt pay hobby to what's being stated, as well as the context wherein it is being said. This includes studying the numerous lines and body language. We additionally cautiously observe matters earlier than we take movement. These trends are all advantages in relationships in sizeable. They can help you build relationships which can be deeper and more potent. Leverage them properly!

Bear in mind which you are more-touchy to external stimuli. If you feel you want to focus all of your interest on what's being said, attempt to minimise outdoor distraction. Request to go to a quiet location. The man or woman you are focussing your hobby on will revel in and respect your sole reputation and fashionable presence.

Do Your Homework or Play Detective

Small communicate - you have to do it. Kahnweiler touts doing all your homework in advance than attending an occasion. If you could, gather a piece intel about a number of the folks who can be there. Formulate a few questions and feedback that you may use as conversation starters or fillers.

If you without a doubt don't apprehend some aspect approximately the human beings attending the event, formulate large questions based totally totally on the event. If it's far a faculty event, ask, "How many youngsters do you have got were given?". You also can carry up some element personal, for example, in case you've just come decrease again from a cruise, percentage your reviews, appropriate or terrible. If you're at a complete loss, listen in on conversations and pitch in while you may.

Buy Time

Kahnweiler says, "A lot of introverts can turn out to be hectic approximately what they must say next in a verbal exchange - plenty just so they omit what the alternative person is saying." You can fill an opening inside the verbal exchange by means of rephrasing what changed into truely stated for your non-public terms. This will show which you're listening and processing what's being said, and buy you time to respond.

Press Repeat and Deflect

Develop a hard and fast of answers to questions that you probable will want to subject, mainly if you are attending a family characteristic or a social feature in which you've no longer visible a few humans for a while. You may also ought to answer questions like, "When are you settling down?" or, "Do you have got someone specific?" again and again inside the direction of the feature, so giving automated answers will save you the mind-drain of arising with smart, however non-committal ones.

Also workout gently deflecting on the equal time because the communique consequences in subjects that you aren't comfortable discussing, like politics.

Work It

Taking on a venture eases the tension of being in a crowd. Busy yourself in any way viable, from bussing tables to handing out drinks or looking after the youngsters. When you are occupied, you won't experience as pressured nor awkward reputation by myself, and you may be a lot much less probably to be imposed upon to make small speak or. You may additionally moreover find like-minded humans as you are going approximately your organisation, and this could cause the greater massive conversations that introverts choose.

Shutdown Time

Understand and be given that you may have moments of shutdown at the same time as you without a doubt need to break out from the crowd, the noise, the conversations and the hustle and bustle. When you experience like you're fading out, slow your breath down and excuse yourself for a while. Helgoe shows, "strive being very despite the fact that, as if you are expecting the other to complete, then looking down or away, that may communicate you're equipped to move on." You can look in advance to a pause in the verbal exchange and make your excuses.

Get some solitude via going to the toilet, out to the balcony, or perhaps fake to make a call. Ten minutes of reconsolidation need to get you decrease lower again onto your social feet.

Also recognize that you have your social limits in which sufficient is sufficient. For a few introverts, one or 2 hours is truely all they may be capable of take earlier than they ought to make their excuses and drift home. Maximise the time you have got were given at an event. Talk to the human beings you really need to, do the crucial, and get out on the equal time due to the fact the going is good.

~Connect~

Making connections is one of the matters that introverts need to make a aware try to acquire. Whether within the social area, relationships, or at faculty or the workplace, you received't get anywhere with out the functionality to connect with people, and you want strong connections with folks who will assist you and assist you to be the tremendous that you'll be.

You in no manner recognise who will make an impact on your existence - it may be the affection of your lifestyles, a casual acquaintance, a client or a chairman. So push through the intellectual barrier and in no manner forestall making connections.

1. One

Remember that we are all certainly already connected; in reality top notch components of 1 big entire. This seems like a hippie-dippy component to say, however if you recollect it, it's actual. We got here from the identical beginnings (the Big Bang, Creation, a few thing you agree with in). We all have trials and tribulations, top notch satisfaction and top notch tragedy. We all are part of Mother

Nature. We all have comparable frame systems. All we need to do is take that one step in addition to make that mental and/or emotional connection. Blaz Kos, private development creator, lifestyles strategist, private teach, begin-up fanatic and online entrepreneur reminds us,

"You don't see the relationship? Very surely: if you clutter the Earth, absolutely everyone is exposed to the harm. If you are making some human beings glad and they make some humans satisfied, you can make an entire u . S . Happy, and numerous glad international locations can advocate a happier planet."

2. What Ice?

Coming from the point of view that there in no way changed into any ice initially, receives you a long manner towards not having to deal with it. If small communicate certainly isn't your difficulty, skip it. You'll absolutely make a better first have an impact on this way - showing which you're cushty enough to not experience the want for preliminaries.

Skipping the small talk moreover manner that you could proper now

start attempting to find a manner to construct a bond. Conversely, if you honestly can't discover commonplace ground, you may bow out graciously while not having spent an excessive amount of time on it.

three. Create Awesomeness

Do things which is probably so thoughts-blastingly brilliant that your recognition will precede you. People will then want to make the connection with you, and they'll be those drawing near you, in desire to the alternative manner round.

Chapter 5

Getting Ahead In the Workplace

Introverts art work better once they have the time and area to work and count on on their private. They generally want order and peace wherein to be revolutionary. When it involves projects and conferences, introverts decide on small corporations and duties that spotlight every individual's competencies, and they may be extra snug getting their message across in writing.

The problem is that the administrative center is typically now not a conducive vicinity for an introvert. The office setup often leaves no room for solitude and there are normal stimulations, interactions and needs, all of which suck strength and slow productiveness, consistent with Cain in an interview with Harvard Business Review. She references a take a look at in which introverts and extroverts were given math issues to clear up at the equal time as historical beyond noise come to be done. The quantity of the ancient past noise modified into grew to emerge as up and down at various periods during the examine, and researchers located that introverts have been at their most powerful at the same time as the noise diploma end up decrease, at the identical time as the opportunity have turn out to be right with the extroverts.

An introvert can maintain their very own within the speedy-paced place of work in the event that they artwork smart and live right to themselves. Cain emphasizes, "We understand that introverts are very creative due to the fact their very propensity for running in solitude and with hundreds of interest genuinely aids in the modern device. When psychologists have looked at who have been the most innovative people over time in a large form of fields, nearly all of the humans they looked at had excessive streaks of introversion, They have been comfortable going off with the aid of using themselves and focusing."

Turn the Camera In

Do a few self-mirrored photograph and take a look at the positions you've held within the past to awareness in your potential set, as well as your faults. Objectively take a look at each, and you'll have a clearer image of what you're able to. Even look at your pastimes to appearance what sincerely makes you tick.

That stated, recognize that introverts have tendencies that make a contribution substantially to the place of work. Cain says, "Introverts are persistent, diligent, and targeted. [They will solve a difficult problem], and they'll art work tougher and longer than extroverts."

There is also a modern advantage for introverts, in step with Cain. "A vital a part of being modern is being able to go off through your self and count on topics thru."

Choose Wisely

"Finding roles that suit you," Cain advises, is one of the vital keys to popping out on top inside the place of business. Since you aren't snug with big quantities of interplay and want an extended time to method it, discover a form of artwork that allows you to be more solitary.

In this factor in time, the idea of 'art work' has come to be loads extra flexible and you can tweak many careers to suit your personality and luxury degree. Even a method like human belongings, in which you are usually required to have interaction with many people all through the day, can be tweaked to in form an introvert's character.

Location, Location, Location

It is going without pronouncing that in which you spend most of your day will have an impact on your happiness and productivity. Many businesses are a exquisite deal more touchy to our emotional needs these days, and you commonly aren't stuck with what you're given, artwork-wise or in terms of place of business place. Negotiate a manner in which you may be powerful in an environment that is snug for you, be it a corner cubicle that's a piece extra shielded, or perhaps at domestic, at your laptop.

If extra secluded everlasting office-area isn't available, search for an opening wherein you can have a few moments of solitude every now and again. You will go back in your table refreshed and charged up.

Take It in Batches

Do comparable responsibilities in batches, like completing all of your administrative art work within the morning, then shift your electricity onto one of a kind topics that may be batched collectively. Introverts attention intensely on a few difficulty, so that they need an prolonged time to refocus their power. By batching, you will up your productiveness at every assignment you do and also you obtained't frazzle your brain.

The Sky Is Not the Limit

An introvert has to tap into their intellectual fitness in addition to their physical health to stay on top. We apprehend what's correct for our our bodies, however we often anticipate we are capable of energy thru with a couple of meetings at a few level inside the day with out a concept as to our intellectual restriction.

Take be privy to how many team tasks you can attend earlier than you start to get frazzled. You can only manage such some of in advance than you need to sit down down and type via all of it to get a address on what desires to be finished. Take a leaf from the pages of LinkedIn CEO Jeff Weiner. He makes certain he regions out his meetings at a few level inside the week in order that he has time every day to manner what grow to be noted and what needs to be completed to transport beforehand.

Listen To Your Intuition

Be in music together with your instinct ... it's going to generally steer you far from needless matters so as to overwhelm you. Remember the eighty/20 rule of productivity wherein eighty% of the effects we churn out are created through the usage of 20% of the artwork we do. Listening for your intuition will manual you far from the unproductive so that you can spend your precious energy at the art work so that you can get the results.

Go It Alone

Get organised and pass it by myself. You have a exceptional potential to blow up with creativity and notion whilst you're allowed to move deep into yourself, but you are very without problems distracted thru any stimuli that intrudes. Do those objects to permit yourself to cognizance:

- Distinguish a few of the urgent, the critical and the trivial. Consciously recognition completely on the pressing first.

- Cut out all distractions. Be very excessive approximately this, as that any small distraction throws you off your undertaking. Even your very very own mind can lead you off beam - as can a mote of dust in the daylight hours ... a line of your chosen tune...

- Develop a productiveness gadget in which you recognition on one undertaking at a time, and preserve on with it in any respect charges. Include such things as writing down thoughts and duties to finish.

-       Snap yourself lower returned to the project to hand with the resource of constantly relating to these system.

-       Allow a certain time for daydreams, then consciously located them on the backburner.

The Right Team

While introverts usually shy away from too much interplay, they might paintings nicely in corporations way to their excessive recognition and functionality to pinpoint the diamond factor amidst the myriad of enter, given the space to recognition.

If you need to work with a hard and fast, try and set up it such that each organization member has a function to carry out inside the route of the very last reason. For an introvert, that is maximum extensively diagnosed to a group that operates on commercial enterprise agency making plans, brainstorming and preference-making.

Introverted lab assistant Taylor Curley shares that he prefers 'cerebral jobs' for which he and his teammates want to remedy complicated troubles on their personal, most effective participating when they have had time to way matters for themselves.

Recharge

It's been said time and time another time, but that's as it's real. Recharging is the important thing to an introvert's success, in anything they do. This is specifically proper at the place of job wherein a nice and calm thoughts-set outcomes in excessive productiveness. Don't fear, "renewal is not for slackers," CEO of The Energy Project Tony Schwartz reassures.

If we have a look at our administrative center surroundings, we comprehend that we're surrounded via a immoderate degree of digital energy, it simply is draining at the maximum extroverted of us. Introverts, in particular, want to step a long manner from this draining energy glide. Schwartz advises in a Huffington Post interview, "We're searching for to preserve up with our era - the virtual go along with the flow operates at this very excessive velocity constantly. Whereas we're designed to perform rhythmically, to move among interest and relaxation; that's even as we're at our nice." So taking a physical spoil from this charged surroundings, similarly to from the chatter and bustle. Take lunch outdoor, or simply bypass for a walk, if possible.

Check In

Introverts is probably greater than inclined to isolate themselves and reputation on their paintings hour after hour. Cain says, but, "We all understand that a part of doing an fantastic hobby is forming the bonds, connections and relationships that anyone need."

Make it a point to take a walk across the place of business every day, preventing to chat with colleagues. At first, you could feel like this is a chore, however in time it's going to begin to be a herbal component. Ignore the niggling enjoy that you're dropping some time. Cain insists that "scheduling in a half of hour or forty five mins an afternoon to do this can skip an prolonged way."

It's particularly essential that you make an effort to regularly take a look at in collectively collectively with your superiors and organization individuals. Do this earlier than they take a look at in with you and they'll reward your initiative.

Medium Should Equal Message

Although you're extra cushty taking images out emails from at the back of your table, recognize that this may now not usually be the extraordinary medium to skip the meant message via. For one problem, keep in mind that humans might not take a look at their emails as regularly as you do. Additionally, if it's a fairly pressing message, you could need to text them, name them, or actually locate the man or woman proper away.

Some interactions certainly need to be face-to-face, so be sensitive to this. I watched a film in which the primary man or woman grow to be a contract downsizing agent. He navigated this touchy minefield with as lots warmth and encouragement as he should, and maximum employees came a ways from the assembly … properly, as a minimum not gutted. A plan changed into put in region to 'modernize' the entire operation, and supply the message via display-chats. You can keep in mind the disaster that ensued.

Finally, half of of of hard work-lifestyles is based totally on the relationships you form alongside side your co-employees and superiors. Relationships can simplest be shaped in character.

Social Media

There is a place for social media in the workplace, however, so don't good buy it. Use a social media internet web web page to pave your manner to a clean meeting by way of way of the usage of introducing your self and offering a touch profile in order that others can get to realise you a chunk without the needful small talk that precedes many gatherings. You also can in advance a few highlights of what's going to be included at conferences, in addition to touching base with clients with whom you've now not been in contact with for a while.

Some introverts normally commonly have a tendency to work higher with the written phrase. If you are considered certainly one of them, leverage this strength. According to Koz:

"In the virtual age, you've got were given numerous options for a manner you can take gain of the capacity to speak nicely in writing as an introvert. You can write articles on systems like Medium, do visitor jogging a weblog, begin your very personal blog, publish slides on SlideShare or answer questions on Quora. Today, you can assemble your non-public brand as an introvert thru producing hundreds of best content material material fabric on particular media platforms."

Game Plan

Always, usually, normally have a undertaking plan before moving into for conferences or discussions. Being organized manner which you gained't experience the strain of bringing up crucial factors on the drop of a dime, and it will additionally make sure which you have treasured contributions to make to the lawsuits. Try to find out the precept elements of the meeting, or maybe what unique attendees will deliver up so you can plan your contributions earlier of time.

Speak Up

Introverts generally communicate softly, but in a assembly, specifically if it's a conference name, you need to make a aware try and task your voice. Your tone of voice furthermore makes an impact. Take care to talk at a measured pace. Speak simply and articulate in a herbal way.

A technique to inject your self into the proceedings is to make your first contribution within the first five minutes of a meeting. It need to absolutely be a remark or query, however it'll make sure that others will see you as present and contributing.

As an introvert, you probably don't speak up too much, so ensure that what you do say is first-rate and impactful. You are likely quite adept at analysing the scenario, so make an effort to achieve this and give you a few factor that makes more revel in than what has already been said. You can also offer a concise precis of all that's been said, presenting the diamond point on a platter which suits brilliantly whilst the meeting goes off-song as conferences every now and then do.

You can also preserve your very personal in competition to the more verbose inside the employer. If you have were given a few issue to function, you could placed your hand up and lightly interject with some component like, "May I say some factor right proper right here."

Idea (Wo) Man

If you've been retaining a word of all the first rate mind that come to you at some point of your quiet introspection time, rent the fact that you are acceptable at analysing, prioritising and making connections, similarly to developing a recreation plan to hold the first-rate mind to fruition.

- Share your thoughts together with your boss, your supervisor, or your organization partners. Even percentage them together together with your pals and own family because you in no manner realize who is probably in a position that will help you develop your mind and convey them to fruition.

- Consider sharing your thoughts online through manner of way of publishing presentations and articles, writing blogs or answering questions and taking detail in discussions.

- Actually plan a course of movement to maintain your ideas to fruition.

-    Hit execute and DO it!

The Diamond Point

Concentration is some different notable characteristic that introverts can be pleased with. You have the ability to approach masses of information and dig out the diamond factors. You can then use the ones diamond factors to make creative connections and formulate knowledgeable guides of movement.

This interest to detail gives you a place due to the fact the satan is in the facts, as they say. You can see what others may additionally moreover have unnoticed. You have a bigger impact whilst you do installed your cents genuinely well worth, and you're able to take care of dangers better.

Chapter 2: Assessing Your Degree of Introversion

What Is an Introvert?

You can also additionally additionally have in no manner been called an introvert within the beyond. Maybe you've got were given completed a surely precise venture of hiding your personal emotions and tendencies. Maybe you are not an introvert and truly are really shy.

Before you get too stuck up on this whole introvert weather, you need to realise what an introvert absolutely is.

The maximum widespread definition of introvert is: a quiet character who does no longer discover it clean to talk to distinct people.

An introvert isn't always a humans individual. The introvert is greater comfortable setting decrease lower again and sticking with parents which can be acquainted. It isn't exactly accurate to mention an introvert isn't always snug talking to one in all a type humans due to the fact speakme to their first-rate buddies and genuinely close to co-people is going to be very clean. In truth, the introvert can also just be the existence of the birthday party whilst it's far those who are close to and familiar.

It is likewise described as a person who makes a speciality of oneself. That makes it sound like an introvert is self-centered in a bad way. That is typically not the case the least bit. An introvert is not stuck-up or self-centered but, due to the fact the introvert chooses to keep away from others or thoughts their personal enterprise, they regularly get categorised as such.

People who see the introvert popularity lower again and best talking to a choose few humans can be dubbed aloof because of the reality they may be now not mingling or making the social rounds.

An introvert isn't going to be the person who walks into a celebration and starts introducing themselves and talking to entire strangers.

The introvert will probable migrate to small businesses of humans with as a minimum one familiar face. An introvert is probably no longer going to be the life of the birthday party on this sort of scenario and could pick out to first-rate talk to the few people she or he is aware of. This is why they will be predisposed to earn the label of being stuck-up.

An introvert is likewise categorized as delinquent. This is a hard one because of the fact, in truth, an introvert is delinquent with the resource of the actual definition, but no longer in the direction of absolutely everyone in sizeable.

It is really the fact they pick out out their very non-public business enterprise. An introvert is probably emotionally drained after spending any period of time in social conditions that require them to talk with others. It isn't always some thing private; it is simply the manner an introvert is harassed out.

Do Your Homework 01

Uh-oh, you did not recognise there has been going to be homework? You had better get used to it, pal, because of the fact each financial ruin can also have its very very personal exercises to perform in order that will help you increase your air of thriller.

Theory is tremendous, however it's the exercising so one can really get you to exchange.

For this number one homework, you could loosen up. All you can want to do is to get a spiral pocket e-book. This pocket ebook is going to be a diary of kinds. You can hold it personal or percent it with a relied on buddy and get their evaluations on what you have were given written after each task.

It is normally enlightening to listen what others keep in mind us. It is often very remarkable than what we do not forget ourselves.

Keep this pocket ebook reachable. Once you are finished with this e-book, you can however need to reference it or hold to work on the numerous sporting activities you could have observed out.

This is your first step to breaking out of the introvert stereotype and embracing a whole new worldwide that you may have formerly idea wasn't possible.

Are YOU an Introvert?

Now you're possibly a touch pressured. Are you clearly an introvert? Are you shy, however clearly an extrovert? Oh, labels are hundreds amusing—no longer!

In this case, a label is okay, due to the fact it is going that will help you maximize your strengths. You can placed in your introvert or extrovert label with pleasure and now not be embarrassed approximately who you're.

Everyone has strengths and simply all people has weaknesses. Being one or the possibility may want to not make you higher. It could no longer endorse you are greater worth of a advertising and marketing at art work and it does no longer advise you are ineligible because of your base character tendencies.

This small tick list will help making a decision whether or not or no longer you are absolutely an introvert or perhaps you're great a bit shy or worrying about being in public. Answer every question in fact.

There is not a wrong answer. Fudging the reality is only going to make it more hard on the way to tap into your strengths.

• You opt to be by myself over spending time in big agencies. A Saturday night time at home at the sofa or doing your selected interest is a long way greater attractive than placing out on the club or going out with friends. You experience your solitude and would instead set off a few song at home on my own and simply relax;

• Being in very public, social placing is physically and emotionally draining. It also can exceptional be a couple hours, but by the point you get domestic you may feel as if you have run a marathon or been up for days. It depletes your electricity absolutely;

• You do no longer usually need to talk at the smartphone or maybe reply to texts. When the phone jewelry, you may forget approximately it or send it to voicemail extra often than no longer. It can also take numerous mins or longer so you can textual content back a pal. The sheer act of speaking while you are on your zone takes a number of electricity that you may no longer continually have;

• Small communicate is draining. An introvert prefers conversations approximately things which might be truly relevant and vital as a substitute then mundane conversations that permits you to be forgotten 5 minutes after they will be performed;

•   You observe matters about your surroundings and people. An introvert is honestly more observant. By now not talking and socializing, you've got got got extra time to take in your surroundings;

•   When in businesses, you are commonly quiet and doing more listening than speaking. You simplest communicate when you have some aspect of fee to function to the verbal exchange;

•   You will be inclined to assume earlier than you talk. You aren't one to fly off the deal with, and you could take several seconds or perhaps longer to reply to a query;

•   You are in all likelihood a chunk standoffish and are not willing to just accept anyone at face price. An introvert wants to assess all of us and determine whether or no longer or not they are sincere and who they certainly say they may be. You are slow to consider;

• You do no longer find out your self sincerely bored very often. An introvert's thoughts is continuously busy considering diverse conditions and making plans. Mulling over beyond and cutting-edge issues is a commonplace manner to pass the time. You may discover you want to take a look at, do puzzles and different activities that permit you that quiet, deep introspect that recharges you;

• Your awesome friend has been your tremendous buddy for a long time. When you're making friends, they'll be lifelong commitments. You now not frequently permit everybody into your inner circle. Rather than having a large institution of pals, you only have a near few which you experience spending time with;

• You are probable the pass-to individual whilst your near buddies want advice. Your capability to investigate and consider a trouble will allow you to suppose via the numerous situations, which makes your recommendation heartfelt and in maximum times, accurate;

• You find out you absolutely need to create. You may not be foxy consistent with se, however you need to apply your creativity to responsibilities across the residence. All of your by myself time gives you all of the time you need to absolutely recall what you need, plus the time to make it display up;

• You aren't huge on social media. You do not want to put it on the market your private existence and prefer to be a silent observer. Some human beings may additionally say you are exceedingly non-public or perhaps a touch mysterious. It is extra that you select to maintain to yourself and do not want or want strangers' critiques about your existence alternatives;

• You have regularly been told you are too excessive otherwise you want to lighten up. This is a common introvert character trait. You are deemed excessive because of the truth you are constantly comparing a scenario. You aren't one to jump in with each feet until you have got were given weighed all the options;

• You want to test and watch an interest earlier than attempting it your self. This might also furthermore study to art work situations. You choose to check what others are doing earlier than diving in. You are watching and studying from them so that you are higher prepared and function found out masses from their errors;

• You opt to invite a few humans to your property for dinner or starting up in vicinity of going to their homes. This offers you the capability to govern the situation more and you are extra snug for your very very personal environment;

• If you are at a noisy celebration or an overly-stimulating state of affairs, you typically tend to drift off. Your thoughts consists of you to an area that is quiet. People will tell you which you have zoned out or ask you in which you have got long long past. It is a self-protecting mechanism which you lease, often unknowingly to help you deal with too much occurring spherical you.

If you can select out with more than 12 of these, you're an introvert. You are someone who's maximum comfortable at home, surrounded through your books and hobbies. Going out to a busy mall, wild events or loud stay performance sports is not your idea of a first rate time.

What isn't always stated above is a number of the perceived downsides to being an introvert. You might also moreover experience like you're continuously being exceeded over for promotions or your mind are not taken seriously, in spite of the reality which you positioned plenty of time into studying and planning every one.

You also can experience like, because of the fact you are not a social butterfly and chatting up the boss or your trainer, you're unnoticed.

You watch as your co-humans and others appear to jump over you and flow into past you, at the same time as you're the only with the best thoughts. You have an tremendous artwork ethic, however you definitely do not flaunt it like others. You do no longer have that smooth manner of speakme or the air of thriller that appears to come lower back lower back so certainly to others. This can lead you to experience left out, neglected and unappreciated.

You want to broaden your air of thriller so your thoughts are heard and you're taken more seriously.

You do not have to be the loudest individual in the room or have the maximum buddies to achieve success. It is not a few aspect more than a mixture of your very robust, amazing introvert man or woman trends blended with a piece air of mystery.

Do Your Homework 02

List out the traits you determined decide which you are certainly an introvert. Think lengthy and tough approximately this.

You can embody subjects that are not at the listing above. As you undergo this e-book, you may in all likelihood find out the dispositions are greater of a symptom of being an introvert and now not usually a defining characteristic.

Keep this list accessible; you're going to be referencing it later.

Chapter 3: What is Charisma and Do You Need It?

Now that you understand for sure you're an introvert or possess introvert inclinations, you can begin transferring in advance.

It is time to begin constructing up your air of mystery so that you can start feeling greater achieved. You will experience greater fulfilled and you may love the manner you're able to talk to others and share your thoughts. We simply installation an introvert is complete of revolutionary thoughts so that you can paintings. The trouble is getting them available and heard.

But, wait. What is air of secrecy?

Charisma, by way of manner of using extremely good definition way; compelling splendor or attraction that can inspire devotion in others.

The Webster's dictionary defines it as; a non-public magic of control arousing particular famous loyalty or enthusiasm for a public parent.

Doesn't that sound magical? Who might not need to possess this form of super? It gives you visions of people setting for your every phrase and inclined to visit bat for you, no matter how ridiculous your idea sounds. This is the extremely good that some humans seem to ooze. They stroll right into a room and all and sundry stops to listen what they have got to mention.

You can also understand this awesome in someone at artwork. Maybe it is your boss. Maybe it's far your sibling who has commonly been capable of enchantment to oodles of pals with out even attempting.

The beauty isn't always necessarily a bodily trait or splendor thru society's requirements.

No, the splendor referenced inside the definition is regarding the soul. A individual's real nature or willingness to assist others is an attractive super as a manner to attract people in.

Charisma is all approximately commanding the eye of others, with out even attempting. Someone who is charismatic might not need to convince every different man or woman to really accept an idea. They have this sort of presence about them that it virtually takes area, in reality.

Is air of secrecy some trouble you want?

Technically, likely now not. Is it useful and a proper trait? Absolutely!

The element is that air of mystery is not generally some thing you're born with. For a few, certain; it looks as if they came out of the womb prepared to appeal anybody that passed through manner of. That would no longer endorse you cannot growth your very own logo of air of thriller that will help you get earlier in lifestyles.

Now, as an introvert you will be pronouncing, "I'm ok with what I honestly have. I do not want a few thing else."

You don't have to set a reason to be a millionaire or to very personal your very very personal Fortune 500 commercial enterprise company. That is not what that is approximately. This is ready you feeling like you're heard. Like you're being taken extensively. Feeling as though you can effect exchange for the better.

And guess what. As an introvert, you're quite able to growing with a existence-changing product. It also can need to also be international-changing. Your introvert tendencies provide you with a modern element that may be missing in extroverts.

They moreover make it viable that allows you to sit and daydream all on my own and keep in mind the numerous strategies you could make subjects better. Take a second to search around you. How many stuff are in your home right this very minute that make your lifestyles much less complex?

We are talking some of the maximum ridiculous subjects, just like the little plastic tips on the surrender of your shoelaces to preserve them from fraying.

Every day, we're blessed to gain the advantages of introverts that have located their thoughts to paintings. Yes, they benefited and, sure, they in all likelihood got rich. It isn't so terrible to achieve fulfillment.

You can be thinking, "No, no, no, I do not need any recognition. I do no longer want people speaking to me and what not." Look, you do not ought to have your face splashed during advertising and advertising and marketing and advertising and magazines. You can even though be you, sitting at home (albeit a miles nicer home) doing what you like most. In truth, you can have extra freedom to hang around at home or in your interest room due to the reality you allowed your charismatic self to get you beforehand and earn you a pleasant profits.

It isn't going to be about coins; I realise. However, fulfillment is often related to cash. It does no longer recommend it has to change you. It furthermore does now not assure you'll really get rich. Personal successes look brilliant for each folks. Your idea of fulfillment won't be much like your satisfactory friend's or maybe your closest sibling's.

A couple of psychologists have placed a few important time and strength into studying aura and the manner it permits or hurts human beings. They have determined charisma is a electricity. Not quite a great power, however a few issue known as a referent electricity.

Referent strength is defined as; have an effect on that you have due to the reality terrific people like and respect you.

Charisma is likewise useful in any social putting. You will enjoy greater cushty talking with others. In reality, your terms is probably listened to and held on. Introverts are such deep thinkers that they nearly constantly have some thing of fee to add to a conversation, however they will be regularly omitted or no longer heard actually because of the truth they do have a tendency to be quiet.

Charisma is the tool you want to simply express your thoughts and critiques.

There are numerous splendid, valid reasons you want and need charisma in your private and expert lifestyles.

•   You will seem confident, so you can finally bring about you feeling confident. Part of the purpose introverts aren't taken seriously is because of the truth they seem timid and shy at the same time as they will be imparting an idea or solution. They do no longer appear to really trust in what they're pronouncing. Charisma gives you that self perception that makes you sound authoritative;

• Charisma gives you the functionality to have interaction others to your mind and making plans. You ought to have the self perception to deliver human beings on board. People will recognize you noticing them and, because of your charismatic presence, they're going to be satisfied to oblige;

• With newfound self perception comes newfound reason. Charisma is a lot like an adrenaline rush. You will see clearer and be capable of recognition really to your project or intention without constantly blockading the relaxation of the sector out. You have a intention and you are decided to obtain it. You had been capable of articulate the goal, which permits breathe existence into it;

• Charisma gives you this magical capability to color a clear photo for others to look. Your use of eloquent phrases that bring your ideas to existence are going to have people flocking to you. They will need to be part of your imaginative and prescient.

Because you're particular, air of mystery might also additionally look a touch in every other way on you than it does on someone else.

We all have our strengths. You may be better at painting the picture of your vision whilst a few particular charismatic person can be better inside the real management vicinity. The key's to recognize your strengths and tap into them. You do not want to be extraordinary at everything, but you do need to have the self belief to maximise the belongings you are extraordinary at.

You may furthermore have an icky feeling about a few charismatic human beings and this is everyday. Some human beings ooze air of mystery and that they use it to their sole benefit. A pushy shop clerk who manages to talk you into looking for some element you failed to want or need can also have air of secrecy in spades, but they may be using it for evil. Well, no longer evil, however they are the use of it to do horrible, in preference to suitable. They are the usage of it to in my opinion get beforehand at the price of someone else.

That isn't always the type of air of mystery you want to broaden or beautify.

Charisma can pass either manner. Let's anticipate you desire to expand your air of thriller to help others at the same time as supporting your self sense better and do higher in the game of existence. It is all about balance. Smooth speakme a bit antique female out of her retirement fund may be an great demonstration of aura, but it is inaccurate. Charisma need for use to better the arena—or as a minimum your little nook of the arena.

Now, you can honestly get ahead or be the chief of your enterprise or the CEO without air of mystery, but it may not be clean. You might not have that knack for uplifting loyalty pretty the equal manner and you may war plenty extra. Charisma isn't just for others. It is for you. It will in addition inspire you and your introverted tendencies to do greater and to be higher. It will give you a healthful dose of self-self perception that will help you smash the limits that each you've got got were given imposed on your self or others have imposed on you due to the fact you've got were given allowed them to.

It is essential you completely apprehend aura and then decide why you want it.

Be cautious you do no longer emulate a person else or determine you want to boom your air of thriller so you can be greater like Bob. Bob won't be as satisfied as he puts on or he can be the usage of air of mystery is a way that is not conducive to your very very own personal beliefs and center values.

Charisma is a tool that could backfire if you use it incorrectly. It is crucial to apprehend that the right manner to use air of thriller is to benefit the humans you are running with or hoping to influence. Charisma isn't always all approximately you. Sorry. You can not make your self the focus of the air of thriller.

Now, if you get up to be a rockstar at the air of mystery element, it is simple to fall into the ego lure of being extraordinarily charismatic. People may be falling at your feet and that could result in you taking the praise and adoration and sidelining the actual cause on your newfound charismatic strategies.

It is ready you influencing others to do better, be higher and enhance in desired.

Do Your Homework 03

On a clean internet web page to your pocket book, write down 5 assets you desire to accomplish through improving and utilising air of secrecy.

These can be small or lofty goals. Some thoughts must encompass:

• Get promoted at paintings based on your excellent simple common overall performance;

• Give a presentation about a new idea you have got;

- Volunteer with a neighborhood business enterprise to help those in want;

- Run for office;

- Apply for a modern-day interest;

- Finish your thesis.

Your desires may be some aspect you have thought about, but have usually assumed you couldn't collect due to the fact you surely did not have the center or have been afraid you'll now not be taken severely.

This is an essential list, so take some time.

If you can not come up with 5 dreams, purpose to have as a minimum 3. This listing is going to be referred to and labored on over the subsequent severa chapters.

Chapter 4: Tap into Your Introvert Strengths

One of the exceptional elements approximately knowing who you truly are is the fact you could tap into those strengths.

Yes, everybody has strengths, virtually as each person has skills they're not so incredible at. Even introverts may be public leaders and a achievement bosses. Their course to the pinnacle is going to appearance a infant-of-a-kind, however it's miles viable.

There are loads of very famous introverts who've changed the arena or who're extraordinarily a fulfillment. They are political leaders and CEOs. Some have even grow to be actors — which, while you keep in mind the traits of an introvert, is difficult to expect.

They were a success because of the fact they have discovered out a manner to apply their introvert traits to their advantage.

There is a huge false impression that being an introvert approach you may constantly be stuck on your dark little cubicle inside the corner, too afraid to come out. Too afraid to speak up or gift your thoughts and critiques.

Introverts aren't meek mice. A higher description can be stealthy. An introvert is not going to be the character shouting and leaping up and all of the way right down to get hobby. No, an introvert is the guy who quietly is going about his business, doing his interest and doing it properly and getting earlier without severa fanfare.

The problem is, bosses word overall performance. Your teachers word superb paintings. People round you will be privy to the person who is effecting change and not sincerely squawking approximately it. That is wherein an introvert will excel. An introvert is a effective strain to be reckoned with, especially once they upload charisma to the mixture.

You may be the massive boss. You may be an ace at what you do. You can be one of the exceptional humanitarians in the worldwide in case you discover ways to use your strengths mixed with a hint air of thriller.

For a few crazy cause, introverts are getting a horrible rap. They can be outstanding leaders. In reality, they're without a doubt super in positions of electricity. Introverts are suitable at their jobs and we are going to undergo some of the motives why.

Prudent Practitioners

One of the principle strengths of an introvert is the ability to make decisions based totally totally on information.

An introvert isn't going to jump into something like a hothead; he will take his time to accumulate facts and run through diverse results based totally mostly on a preference before definitely pulling the motive.

This makes them pleasant leaders due to the truth they'll be no longer going to make any knee-jerk picks that would be encouraged through manner of instantaneous rewards.

Introverts have a observe the large picture and might be willing to place within the time and work to honestly prevail. They are not going to be with out issues influenced with the aid of the usage of those who are searching for to push their personal agendas.

Fabulous Listeners

One best notable in any leader is the ability and willingness to concentrate to others. You can study masses through shutting your mouth and beginning your ears.

Haven't we been informed that for the purpose that first day of college? Turns out our mother and father and teachers have been right. You aren't some final being who is aware of the whole thing. Sorry, however it is a fact. Taking the time to concentrate to others and gather enter from a group or a fixed of different professionals is an invaluable skill.

Introverts are really large on sitting again, listening and soaking up records. They do not have to tell all and sundry their opinions or beliefs. They apprehend them and that is all that topics. The secret's paying attention to others and matching those evaluations and mind as lots as what you think to be actual and, from there, evaluating what is in fact the exquisite choice.

Think of it as a massive hodgepodge of statistics. The introverted mind will quietly sift via all of it and characteristic it make revel in.

Creative Beings

Introverts are modern. That would now not suggest all introverts are Mozart or Picasso. Creativity is to be had in all paperwork. Introverts can provide you with a few unique, innovative thoughts about problem solving and severa strategies to inspire humans due to the reality they revel in sitting, questioning and thinking of.

For some introverts, they in reality are craft kings and queens in a physical feel. Others can be storytellers. It is all about tapping into the mind and focusing greater on what is inner your head as opposed to seeking out amusement in the out of doors worldwide.

A innovative chief goes as a way to check troubles with a completely open thoughts. They are not going to be limited via what has always been finished. An introvert is going to have a look at a situation, mull it over, listen to enter and suppose outdoor of the sphere. This is how problems are efficaciously solved.

Humble Humans

One of the maximum critical and most applicable traits of an introvert is their humility. They are humble people. They are not afraid to take recommendation from others. They are inclined to take note of absolutely everyone who gives a few shape of rate. They make the effort to investigate names and pay attention to the humans they paintings with and spend time with.

Introverts are very observant. They are going to understand the signs of someone feeling disappointed. This may be an worker, a patron, a co-employee or the man repute on the road nook. This is one of the introvert inclinations that tends to draw people in. It is air of mystery in its great shape.

People don't care to be spherical or lend aid to smug, self-absorbed folks that do not supply a fig about others. People need to comply with someone they apprehend. Your introvert tendencies are admirable and nicely well worth of being respected however, because of the truth you are so humble, you can not permit every body inflate your ego. Introverts aren't susceptible. They are not usually timid. Just due to the truth someone is pretty quiet and continues to himself does no longer make that person prone. You, the introvert, have many effective strengths at the manner to make you an extremely good chief, and you may add air of secrecy to those tendencies with a piece attempt.

Yes, it's going to experience a touch weird at the begin however, while you understand that aura does no longer require you to set out on a route to worldwide recognition, you'll see it's far very useful to you and people you'll in the end encourage.

The inclinations indexed above are that of an introvert and of a charismatic man or woman. It is your approach to combination the 2, which you may look at the manner inside the direction of the course of the e-book.

Do Your Homework 04

Grab your notebook and write down at the least five of your strengths. This list may additionally moreover moreover appearance similar to the list of attributes in the first section. That's okay. This may be extra difficult for some. Now, this list is going to be greater mainly associated with the ones introvert developments we have been talking approximately.

In this financial ruin we included the various traits and the way they have been really strengths that would help you turn out to be a pacesetter or more charismatic in elegant. Your strengths also can truly be at the listing of tendencies of an extrovert. That is adequate. There isn't anybody-length-suits all. Your area of expertise is what makes you precise and will bring your very personal particular logo of air of mystery to the table.

Chapter 5: Go On a Path of Self-Discovery

This is an essential step on the street to building your air of thriller. Too often, we get caught up with the way subjects have continuously been or human beings telling us who we're, what we love and what we are correct at, and we truly take transport of it. They appear like proper and it seems to healthy, so why restore what isn't broken?

Unfortunately, it's far an extended way too clean to get into that consolation quarter and in no way push the limits to check ourselves. Introverts get so snug at home or in their same uninteresting undertaking with the humans they have got labored with for some time, they do no longer need to project the status quo.

You may additionally moreover sense happy. You are glad with the manner your lifestyles is—for the maximum component.

Have you ever had those moments in which you longed for some element else? Have you decided yourself waking up within the morning, laying there a minute and wondering: right here we circulate yet again?

You possibly have. That is due to the fact your life has turn out to be mundane. It had end up one large grind, day in and day trip, and however you're too afraid to exchange it. Change may additionally want to advise failure, and failure is lousy, right?

Wrong! Failure is remarkable! Failure way you attempted and it did now not pretty worked out as deliberate, but you determined out from that experience. You got a flavor for a few component a touch unique. That is invigorating. That makes you feel alive. You can typically strive again and examine from those mistakes.

You don't know what you need till you strive. You do now not recognize what you really need till you carry out a touch self-discovery.

When you are someone who's sincerely satisfied and obsessed on every new day, it's going to show. It united statesyour air of mystery. People are going to be interested by that internal mild that looks to glow internal.

Introverts can stay thrilling lives. An introvert would no longer want to be the guy at home on the sofa on a Saturday night because human beings are simply now not his issue. There are one hundred different things that fit into the introvert manner of life that are not socially draining.

Without further ado, permit's display you how to flow for your personal route of self-discovery. This will assist you discover your passions and to amplify your horizons.

You will revel in more happy, confident and function lots of factors to talk about in relation to making small talk.

For this phase, it is probably a exceptional concept to use the pocket e book you have got got been completing your homework duties in.

1-Do a piece loose writing

Write down your hopes and goals. Let them flow. They can be quite lofty and perhaps even a long manner-fetched. That's adequate.

Write them down. Think about in which you need to move, what you want to try to who you need to satisfy. Even introverts have people they recognize.

Write down desires you could have, like developing a brand new invention or locating a way to quit homelessness. Whatever crosses your mind, jot it down.

These mind and goals are revealing who you are and your innermost passions.

2-Now, searching at those mind and goals...

Start making a listing of why you can't obtain your dreams. Be sincere. It's k. This is in truth loose questioning and a loose float of mind. Sometimes, it helps to surely see what we are thinking so we're capable of pass about organizing those mind.

This method lets in us give you a plan. If you need to, you may ask a close to buddy to present you their enter on why they do not count on you can benefit your hopes and dreams. This step also can look like a temper killer, however it is meant to make you face your demons.

You are looking at the negativity head on. It would not look quite so frightening while it's miles on paper and also you apprehend how ridiculous or unfaithful pretty some the ones little demons surely are.

three-Okay, now with the icky factor out of the way...

Let's begin to remove all that negativity with a few excellent statements and moves. Start listing all the trends you personal that make it possible that allows you to meet those goals.

Again, ask a friend to help you out and provide you with their opinion in case you are snug with it. In the very last chapter, you wrote out your strengths. You can comply with those here, however you furthermore mght want to put in writing down down down more that pertain to your desires mainly.

four-Okay, allow's pass again to the first step

Read that listing again. What is the simplest or maybe two topics that supply a tear in your eye or make your heart beat a chunk quicker at the concept of actually doing it?

Write it down.

If you have got a couple, use those, but the secret is to in fact recognition on one or items. They can be very comparable, like feeding the homeless and supplying the homeless with an area to sleep. Those pass hand in hand and are essentially one major motive.

We are walking in the direction of locating your lifestyles reason or what you recognize your cause in life to be. This one problem is what is going to get your blood pumping. It will make you passionate. It will give you the braveness to fight for it and you will find out you may need to talk with whole strangers about this one reason in your lifestyles.

This is wherein your aura is going to begin to definitely shine.

five-At this element, you have to be feeling excited

Energy should be thrumming thru your veins. You definitely had your a-ha second and your mind might be in overdrive thinking about how thrilling it might be to sincerely fulfill that dream.

Sit tight for a minute. It is time for a bit greater self-discovery that will help you super-song that purpose in life. Grab your pocket e-book and list out your middle values. This may be as an opportunity prolonged, so summarize if need be.

Your middle values can be such things as: you could never cheat, your family is the maximum essential part of your lifestyles, you desire to assist, you are kind, you're beneficiant, and so forth.

This goes to be a hard one due to the fact they're quite a few who you're, it is difficult so you can truly choose out the ones developments.

It is a amazing idea to invite more than one pals their evaluations approximately what they accept as true with your middle values to be.

6-Now which you have all of this information in the front of you

You need time to procedure. Do a few thing it's far you do whilst you want to mull over a problem or reflect onconsideration on a task. Go for a walk, circulate for a hike, hang out at domestic for the night time time.

You simply uncovered lots of facts and also you want time to method all of it. Ride that power buzz this might be coursing via your veins.

Jot down more mind that come to you so you can artwork them into the puzzle you have got got simply created. Every piece leads you one step in the direction of your cause.

7-Now which you have processed all of the facts and grow to be greater enlightened approximately who you are and what motivates you...

You can start to attention your electricity on fascinating your existence's purpose. You are going to fulfill new folks that percentage your passion for a undertaking. Your air of secrecy goes to be actually charged at this point and you may discover it is straightforward to talk with others who percentage your hobbies.

They won't be pretty as passionate as you are, but you will inspire them and they will observe your lead because of the fact your air of mystery is going to be taking up. Let it.

You must be feeling truely top proper now. Like a veil has been removed from your eyes and also you sense as though you may see in reality. You have uncovered the thing that motivates you and you are equipped to pursue it. You have a purpose.

Purpose is what gets us up each day and gets us inspired to cope with new problems and goals.

Do Your Homework 05

Take everything you've got located approximately your self and offer you with a plan to attain your cause.

Start small. Take the listing of things which might be keeping you lower lower lower back and flow into them off one after the alternative with the resource of changing them with fixes or workarounds so that you can obtain your goal.

If it is a lack of time, make the time. If it's miles a lack of motivation, you probably already fixed that via envisioning your self completing your intention or operating within the route of your life purposed.

This is a web web page you will preserve with you for a while. As you acquire each of the smaller desires you've got got set which can be getting in the direction of the main reason, reward yourself for a assignment nicely executed. Keep moving in advance and incorporating help from others by using the usage of using your newfound air of mystery capability.

Look the Part

You might not want to be a notable version or the winner in a most adorable contest, but you do want to have some issue called presence.

Of course, "presence" has no longer some thing to do with being present at a meeting or in a room. "Presence" is about people information you're there. People check while you stroll in.

They may additionally take their cues from you as they secretly watch your response to matters being stated or a presentation.

Presence is just like the moon inside the sky. It does no longer something, but we all understand it's miles there.

Presence is set you being attentive to what is taking place spherical you or the individual you're having a communication with. You are present and attentive. You aren't scribbling in a pocket e-book or looking over the individual's shoulder, mulling over what you can watch on tv whilst you get home.

You are in the 2d. Giving a speaker your entire interest is something they may observe. They will respect your willingness to concentrate them out.

When we say look the detail, we are speakme about that cognizance. You want to make eye touch with the speaker. Keep your shoulders again and your fingers even though.

Gently leaning into someone if it's far a one-on-one verbal exchange is some different manner to expose them they have got your entire attention. Put the cellphone down. Put the pencil down and do now not make small speak even as a person is talking.

These little subjects lead us to our next difficulty—frame language.

Your body language will say plenty approximately you. If you need to appear like listening and giving a person your complete interest, you need to make certain your frame says it.

You do not need to interrupt a person to allow them to realize you are listening. When you stroll proper into a meeting or even as you sit down down collectively with your boss or interview for a method, one manner to apply your air of mystery is to be virtually gift.

Make wonderful you're properly rested. You do no longer want to be yawning, stretching or drifting off. That isn't always charismatic. In fact, it's miles shape of rude. That sort of body language says you may care heaps an awful lot less approximately the individual, the agency or what is being stated. If you're focusing and appealing, you can no longer want to worry approximately those yawns sneaking up on you. You may not need to fear about your mind drifting to more captivating subjects.

Active listening skills are critical to your development of air of secrecy. You need to recognize a manner to portray you care and are attentive. It have to no longer be too tough in case you study the above guidelines.

Some number one strategies to use body language to reveal you're actively being attentive to someone are listed below.

•   Smiling is one way to reveal you are listening to what a person is announcing. It desires to be actual. Cheesy, fake smiles are smooth to perceive and the man or woman doing the talking is going to apprehend you are not clearly paying interest;

•   Posture turned into referred to earlier. Slightly leaning forward or if sitting at a desk, propping one's chin within the palm of their hand is likewise a manner to show you are actively listening. This allows keep you from fidgeting and sends clear alerts you are surely listening;

•	Mimicking the speaker's expression is normally involuntary in case you are in segment collectively together with her. You will smile once they smile, tear up inside the event that they tear up and appear amazed if their eyes widen. This tells the speaker you are right there inside the second with them;

•	Nodding and making small sounds of settlement or gasps at surprising bits of the tale are also telltale signs and symptoms and signs and symptoms you are giving them your entire and undivided interest.

Part of looking charismatic is with the resource of manner of defensive yourself in a way that demonstrates you have got got self perception.

For a few, this can be a piece difficult. You may be an introvert, but you could moreover be a little timid. The majority of human beings on this global, whether or no longer they may be introverts or extroverts, are a chunk uneasy in massive crowds. It is human nature. The secret's to fake you're confident and ultimately your brain will buy into the ruse.

Although you could now not be all that excited to talk publicly or perhaps to be found, you want to be prepared certainly in case you are.

Your posture is a large deal. When you think about those who are charismatic, you regularly count on they will be confident. They have a manner about them that makes them appear to be they may be cushty in their very private pores and skin and glad to be who they may be.

One instance of this demonstration of self warranty can be celebrities taking walks red carpets. They strut, smile, wave and deign to speak to journalists.

Politicians on marketing campaign trails do the same and could shake palms and make small communicate with severa human beings. It is curious about show. It is supposed to hook up with the humans they may be hoping to influence.

You don't ought to go to such extremes, but take a look at out some of the techniques you can help exude air of mystery and in the long run start to enjoy it.

• Hold your head up, shoulders once more and chest out. Good posture makes you look like you revel in incredible and it does without a doubt make you feel greater assured. Walk in like you are in rate. People be conscious those subtle hints. Don't slouch;

• Make eye contact with people while you stroll in or while you're seated. If you are at a podium, discover some quality faces, make eye touch and smile;

• Dress for fulfillment. If you appearance well, you enjoy correct. You do not have to shop for designer apparel or new clothes. Take what you have, ensure it's miles in real shape. Iron your apparel if wanted. Add accessories to make the outfit look smarter. Dressing brilliant does not need to price a fortune. Don't walk about in grimy garments or garments which you do not enjoy assured in;

• Shake fingers with people. This is a outstanding manner to say precise day and brings virtually all people proper all of the way right down to the equal stage. For a few interactions, a hand at the shoulder is suitable;

• Keep your arms from your wallet! It is quite hard to shake palms or touch someone's shoulder if your fingers are hiding to your pants. The act of contact is charismatic and lets in humans revel in associated with you. Plus, it is tough to maintain your shoulders once more in case your palms are in your pockets;

• Avoid setting your hands for your mouth. Don't chunk your nails! This may be translated in masses of superb techniques;

• Don't shuffle while you stroll. Pick up your toes and take prolonged, assured strides. Again, it's miles all approximately supplying yourself in the nice feasible slight. People are going to be drawn for your self notion;

• Pay hobby on your personal hygiene. Go smooth on the cologne or fragrance. Make sure your breath smells right and your hair is in order. Again, you do not need to have a $100 haircut, simply look the part of someone who's attentive to their appearance. Carry deodorant with you if the pressure of public conditions has an inclination to make you sweat extra;

• Always smile. People might be drawn to you. A smile says you're approachable.

This is one step on the way to take a few workout. The extra you do it, the higher you can get and the much less hard it'll be. You will enjoy the alternate inside the manner you enjoy at the identical time as you exude self guarantee.

Do Your Homework 06

You do not need your pocket ebook for this one. Practice your confident look in the mirror. Get comfortable with yourself, smiling, nodding and running closer to proper posture.

If you aren't sure there can be a distinction, draw near your cell telephone and take more than one selfies. One with terrible posture and no smile and every other one the usage of the pointers mentioned above. You will see the distinction.

You moreover need to exercise your active listening capabilities. This can be collectively along with your accomplice, your pal or perhaps your 2-one year-vintage. Get into the addiction of the usage of those competencies so they come glaringly to you. If you want to, file yourself having a communique with a person. Watch it and discover the belongings you do or do now not try this you may work on.

Keep It Small

You recognize your limits. As an introvert, you are not going to do properly speakme in front of loads of humans. You will freeze and no person gets to pay attention what you have got to mention. You are entire of precious records and the world may want to surely be a higher region if you can percentage your mind; properly, as a minimum your little nook of the sector may be.

Don't set yourself up for failure by trying to address greater than you can deal with. You will simplest freak yourself out and become walking home for canopy.

You are going to artwork first-rate in small agencies. Let's say you're the CEO of a massive company with masses of employees. You do no longer need to sit down down down with they all on the equal time. Set up conferences with small agencies. This is a greater intimate accumulating and you could revel in more relaxed.

You do no longer must strive to speak or meet with the entire company or the entire department in a unmarried sitting. It isn't always simplest you that is going to revel in intimidated. You aren't the only introvert.

By going with smaller corporations, the opposite introverts might also have a risk to specific their very own thoughts and emotions. You, collectively along side your newfound air of mystery, are going to lead them to enjoy like they are able to. Like they're in a comfortable region wherein thoughts will bring about healthy, massive discussions. They are going to realize the fact that a person is in reality listening.

Just via using keeping those smaller organizations, you are upping your charisma level. The intimacy of a small agency makes you one of the institution. Your lively listening talents are going to make you a valuable member of the agency and you'll find out they gravitate towards you extra.

If you are in massive corporations, people might not see you or listen your enter. Not handiest will you be a wonderful deal much less inclined to talk up, however there can be such pretty some others providing their very very personal two cents, you could without difficulty be drowned out. Now, as your air of secrecy potential will growth, this may lessen due to the truth humans will save you and be aware of what you've got to mention.

Now, irrespective of the fact that you may do exceptional in smaller agencies, do not permit it come to be your safety blanket. There might be times you want to be in large companies. You may be at a party, on the mall or in a few one-of-a-kind social setting that makes small organizations now not feasible. The key's to work that air of secrecy for your gain. You will feed off the charisma and sense greater confident even as those conditions do rise up.

When we are pronouncing keep it small, we also are concerning each day social interactions. You do no longer generally ought to go out of your manner each unmarried day to exercise your charisma skills. Little such things as speaking to the individual making your coffee, the person on the force-thru window or on the grocery preserve checkout. These are clean because of the reality they can't final greater than a minute or . It is genuinely you pronouncing pinnacle day, imparting up a praise or asking a question, they solution and you pass on.

It is you training your air of mystery on the identical time as being sociable and kind to others.

Do Your Homework 07

Grab your pocket e-book. Jot down a time even as you felt along with you have been without a doubt part of a hard and speedy and had been capable to speak up and provide your critiques and suggestions.

Think about why you felt cushty to acquire this. Did you recognize the people surely nicely? Was the business enterprise pretty small? Were you confident about the problem?

Now recollect a time in which you had plenty you desired to say, but did now not. What held you lower again?

Hopefully this exercise is going to show you the difference amongst agency sizes and your confidence stage. Once you have got recognized the subjects that held you over again and what labored exceptional, you may installation your subsequent conferences to be more a success.

Chapter 6: Recuperate and Recharge

Never forget about your introvert goals. If you are in a hectic place of business or you're in an active event, do not allow your self come to be crushed. This will zap your air of thriller. You will appearance compelled and dive into your shell, blockading out truely absolutely everyone spherical you. This is going to make you seem closed off and people aren't going to want to be around you, talk to you and in fact now not want to comply with you. Your opinions is probably silenced with the useful useful resource of your frazzled appearance.

You want to take care of yourself. The care and feeding of an introvert is pretty clean. An introvert goals downtime. Quiet time away from human beings is like recharging your cell cellular telephone battery. Don't push your self beyond your abilties.

You are an introvert and this is okay. No one is saying you need to be available peopling 24/7. It is critical for your survival that you get a couple of minutes inside the direction of the day to just sit decrease lower back.

Recuperating and recharging are going to be a should. If you're crazy busy and over-scheduled all day, the ones quick time of downtime are going to be vital. Pencil them in—regardless of what. If you do not recharge, you will be worn-out and no longer able to feature. You aren't going so one can use your air of mystery let alone expect right away. You are going to be burdened and in all likelihood snap at people. Your reputation as a chunk of a go through will take an lousy lot longer to overcome than your popularity as a charismatic leader.

How you recover can be excellent from a few other introvert. We all have our particular methods of centering ourselves and pulling ourselves decrease back together. Some thoughts that could assist are as follows:

•   Close your office door. Turn off the phone. Give your self 5 or 15 minutes, something works for you. Just take a seat for your workplace gathering your thoughts. Maybe play your selected game for your phone or have a look at a financial destroy out of a e-book you have been reading on my own at home;

• Take a short stroll throughout the block. Yes, you can see human beings on the sidewalk, however you aren't available trying to talk with them. You are simply gambling the clean air and are on my own at the side of your mind;

• Grab your magazine and circulate sit down in a relaxation room stall, a quiet region within the lobby or in your workplace. Write. Introverts are massive on writing and this can serve as a dumping ground. Release all of the ones thoughts and feelings that have been building up within the route of your interactions at a few degree within the day;

• Pop to your earbuds and placed on your favored music. Close your eyes and get cushty. Allow yourself to sit back collectively

collectively together with your thoughts and close to out the place for a few minutes;

• Depending on the scenario, bypass for a pressure. You can force for 20 mins or a couple of hours. Whatever you need. Get a ways from unique people for a bit and just loosen up;

• If you have were given a particular hobby, allot yourself a advantageous amount of time in the day to artwork on it. Allowing your innovative juices to go with the flow permits to take away all of that terrible strength that has an inclination to build up at the same time as an introvert has to engage with humans for prolonged periods of time. Knitting, writing, stitching, whittling, a few factor it's miles that locations you in that Zen state;

• Exercise. This may be to your treadmill at domestic or simply doing some yoga within the park or at home. Gyms are not best places for a exercise for an introvert who desires to recharge. There are too many folks that can also want to talk. You need to close down for a bit.

Going returned to yoga, that is an exceptional way for an introvert to in fact unwind and recharge. Yoga combines meditation with deep respiration and exercising. All of which help recharge the frame physically. The electricity expended at a few degree inside the exercising will assist you center your self. Many of the poses can be executed to your place of job. A few deep breaths blended with a few aspect like the solar salutation will right away make you enjoy higher.

If you are in a excessive stress situation, those deep, cleansing breaths you observe in yoga will flow a long way to assisting you loosen up out and take it all down a notch.

Your potential to stay calm and cool is going to present you more air of mystery factors. People are going to take their cues from you and, in case you are the boss or appeared because of the reality the chief, you want on the manner to calm topics down. Once you've got were given calmed the organization down, you can head off to a quiet nook to absolutely recharge. It is essential you contend with yourself. Don't placed your self into annoying situations with an entire lot of human beings 7 days every week.

You need an afternoon to hang around at the couch or to move off into the woods. Don't e-book your agenda to the issue you barely have time to squeeze in by myself time. This will burn you out and pretty literally make you loopy. You may not have the staying power or the power had to cope with human beings.

You may additionally moreover have a short fuse or shut down altogether.

Do Your Homework 08

Jot down a number of the matters that make you enjoy maximum snug. Whether this is analyzing a ebook, going for walks on a interest or chilling out at the side of your preferred tune on, write it down.

Now, you'll need to decide out how you may make that portable so that you can deliver it with you to artwork. This getting better is best essential for prolonged days at work or spent with others. You do not want to devise on taking your knitting out to the membership or to a party. These restoration recommendations are for those times you want to be faraway from your private home for hours on surrender.

Chapter 7: Developing Your Self-Confidence

Everything we've long lengthy beyond over results in an growth in self-self perception. Many introverts lack self belief, not lots in their very very own information or talents, but in sharing them with others in huge organization settings.

When you're confident, air of thriller has a tendency to ooze from every pore. However, there may be a terrific line among being confident and being conceited.

There are many tactics you can paintings on your self-confidence so that you feel more snug within the ones socially awkward conditions. This will help you beautify your charismatic techniques, and greater humans will concentrate on your terms and be interested in you.

Some of the fastest methods to enhance your everyday self belief stage are as follows:

• Know your stuff. This is an smooth one for an introvert who will spend an entire lot of time studying, studying, evaluating and mulling over all the statistics. Before you head right right into a meeting, brush up on what's going to be blanketed. If you're assured and you are organized, you will sail through it. People are going to be seeking to you for the solutions. This is one way air of mystery is born;

• Look relevant, sense real. Refer returned to the looking the element segment. This is a self perception booster;

• Adopt a high super outlook. Introverts are very realistic and can from time to time get caught up in their private head. They see a problem for what it's far and can inadvertently undertake a totally gloomy mind-set in place of looking for methods to positively impact a situation. Stop the negative thoughts and replace them with a pleasing outlook. Block out the cannots and replace them with cans;

• Be type to others. This makes you experience all warm temperature and fuzzy at the internal and offers you some extreme aura cred. Smile, open doorways, offer a type word or some aspect someone goals in the second. This makes you revel in better in addition to the person you are treating with kindness. Kindness is contagious and you may speedy have an impact on a movement which, another time, usayour air of thriller degree;

• Perfect that posture we cited in advance. Good posture is a photograph of self guarantee. You might also even breathe greater without problem, so that you can make you enjoy higher;

• Set small goals for your self each day and make sure you accomplish them. This can be some thing from cleansing out the junk drawer to writing a letter to someone you haven't talked to in some time. Achieving little desires boosts your self perception and you may quickly be setting large goals and virtually developing your self belief diploma.

You won't suppose you've got have been given any troubles at the side of yourself guarantee degree and you may no longer, but do you painting that during your each day existence?

Introverts have a propensity to be wall flowers and not supply plenty of interest to themselves, they could appearance meek and people can also furthermore assume they lack self notion. People aren't going to be aware of the person who might not keep in mind what they may be announcing.

You have to speak with authority and keep yourself in a way that exudes self warranty.

Do Your Homework 09

Grab your pocket book and write out the times of the week. For each day, set a small motive. It may be tidying up your bookshelf, cleansing up your interest location, exercise or some issue.

Set goals and, while you complete them, positioned a pleasant huge take a look at subsequent to the item. Boom! Your self perception will broaden and you could get that rush of pride at completing a purpose.

Next week, set greater goals, stretching your self a bit greater.

Chapter 8: Stepping Out of Your Comfort Zone

This is the component introverts dread. For a few, it could make you physical unwell to even reflect onconsideration on stepping out of your comfort area with all of your creature comforts.

You may additionally want to rush lower back home to the safety of your couch, with all the ones subjects that rejuvenate you and make you revel in the maximum at peace. It is scary and intimidating in advance than the whole lot, however you need to stretch your self so you can increase. Acting the same manner every single day will exceptional yield comparable effects. If you want to increase and enhance who you're, you need to stretch your self a little bit at a time.

This is probably the maximum difficult monetary disaster inside the ebook, but remember it like this: the larger the task, the extra the praise. This is a need to-do to decorate your air of secrecy and control capability and to extend as a person. If you do not push your self, you get stagnant. You lose interest and complacent. Life can be silly. All human beings crave excitement. It is what receives our juices flowing and genuinely makes us revel in alive. There is being alive after which there can be dwelling.

You want to be within the latter magnificence.

Working by way of manner of your self and covering every inch of research for your non-public is your flow into-to fashion. It has normally labored for you and you do no longer need to exchange. However, you need to. You are a precious asset and others need to apprehend you a hint better and art work with you in the direction of a purpose.

You in all likelihood do now not want to speak in front of 20 to 30 human beings however, again, it's far some issue you need to do from time to time. You do not want to do it every day or maybe weekly, however there are times at the same time as you want to step out of your box and speak out.

You need to chit chat with co-personnel. You need to mingle at a party—even for a fast even as.

Each of these gadgets is going to zap you of your power and you may need to recharge. Think of it as training that an elite athlete need to do. You get available, you train and you then definitely rest and recharge. You get available and you train a touch tougher and get higher results, rinse and repeat. Every time you step out of your comfort location, it'll get a hint much less hard. Make high-quality you address yourself as quickly as you have got driven your self in your limits. Give yourself that downtime you want to rejuvenate.

Don't get crazy and time table another time to once more public speakme engagements. You aren't doing anybody any specific. Push yourself, take a wreck after which skip at it once more whilst you're equipped.

If you've got any critical doubt approximately your functionality to address some thing so far from your comfort zone, get a few help.

There are a few actions you could located into movement on the way to make it a piece an awful lot less complicated to step out of your comfort area and interact with more human beings similarly to big crowds.

• Take a public talking path at your neighborhood network university. These are less highly-priced publications which might be typically simplest a night time time in step with week for a couple hours on every occasion. The courses can provide you with some precious hints and hints to speaking in the front of others in addition to some arms-on exercise. As an introvert, you are huge on amassing data. This is the suitable manner to do this;

• Join a Toastmasters enterprise. This is an incredible, low-fee organization that permits you to art work in your public talking and manipulate talents. There are dues required, however it is very low priced. You receives to sweep up on your public talking abilities and get treasured comments on how you could enhance. This will help assemble your self notion diploma and make stepping out of doors of your comfort location a chunk less complicated;

• Practice speakme or giving a speech inside the the front of a replicate. You also can experience silly earlier than the entirety, but speaking to yourself is steady. You gets to appearance what others are seeing. You will discover ways to stand, what to do along side your fingers and what you appear like in today's. This revel in allows you to restore some problem you determined isn't always quite proper. Maybe you need to fashion your hair otherwise or put on a completely unique outfit;

• Record yourself giving a speech and then watch it. You gets to pay interest your voice, the price at which you are talking and your gestures. Are you searching down at your notes? Are you looking proper away on the camera or away? Assume the camera is your goal marketplace or the individual you're talking to. Keep enhancing and recording till you're confident with the manner you look and sound;

• Give a small presentation for your circle of relatives participants or near friends. This will assist break the barrier of speakme in the the front of small groups. Ask for remarks and what you could change to be better, extra approachable or to appear greater real. Being proper is a cornerstone of air of mystery.

When you step from your comfort vicinity a piece, you could experience demanding.

Push thru the nerves and, on the identical time as it is over, circulate home or discover a quiet vicinity to get higher. While you are chilling out, you're going to mull over what clearly befell. This is a terrific time to congratulate your self for taking the massive step and, of route, undergo a piece self-introspection.

Think approximately what you need to change for the subsequent time.

Do Your Homework 10

Decide what's most critical for you as far as your air of mystery level is involved. Do you want to be able to speak to new people a piece less complicated or are you hoping to cope with a control function at artwork?

When you outline your aim, you want to do one of the following or each.

Step from your comfort location by using introducing yourself to a person at a celebration. Have a organized intellectual list of questions or subjects you could communicate about in your small speak verbal exchange. It does no longer should be extended and also you do now not have to talk for hours. This is actually you stepping out of your comfort region.

If your purpose is to be extra of a pacesetter at paintings, write a speech about a task or write out a faux presentation.

Give the presentation to a hard and fast of pals or document your self giving it. Take be privy to what you in all likelihood did splendid and what you may decorate immediately to be more authoritative.

Uplift Others

One of the biggest mistakes each person can ever make is to fall into the gossip lure. Being overly judgmental is a few other downfall that many, many human beings succumb to.

It is human nature, o.K., however it's miles sad no matter the truth that. We have a propensity to choose apart others in an effort to sense higher approximately ourselves. We need to supply different people down, so we are not by myself in our personal distress. Misery loves agency, or maybe an introvert may additionally moreover be a part of within the pity occasions.

To placed it obviously, it sincerely isn't cool. It is in truth pretty advocate to rip someone down. Nobody is privy to what trials and tribulations any other individual has prolonged lengthy long past via. Nobody is aware of a person's real tale. Picking apart a person for the manner they appearance, speak or perhaps their picks serves no motive. It does no longer something. It does now not assist the vicinity and it does now not make you or the individual being picked on any better.

It is time to prevent.

A charismatic character is someone unique human beings respect and could comply with. A charismatic man or woman is someone who is definitely type to others and works difficult to widely recognized all. Charisma is set anyone feeling a touch particular. Tearing a person down, mocking or gossiping about some different character could not be similarly from air of mystery.

In order to beautify your air of thriller degrees, you want to make it a dependancy to uplift others. You need to be someone who's kind and beneficiant. Generous ought to not constantly propose giving absolutely everyone cash. It may be a few aspect like giving it sluggish through paying attention to their issues or giving it sluggish and electricity by way of the use of way of helping them whole a task.

Generosity can look many terrific methods. It is all about giving to others, although it's miles excellent a grin or a hug.

The following guidelines will help you increase your aura as you uplift others. People will enjoy as when you have bestowed an honor on them without a doubt thru the use of someone of those small gestures. It will motive them to enjoy as although someone cares and that they do rely.

• Ask meaningful questions about the equal time as protecting eye contact at the same time as you meet someone. This may be while you stroll into work ordinary or possibly visit your preferred corner market. The stylish "how are you?" will suffice, however you'll earn extra charisma factors in case you make it a more actual question. Things like, "How did you do at your occasion?" or "How did little Johnny do in football?" These are obviously questions which can be intended especially for an man or woman and no longer common;

• Use someone's call. This goes to take some strive. As you walk via the administrative center door, greet anybody by way of manner of call. Use this trick while you visit regularly visited locations. People will enjoy as although they matter if you keep in thoughts their name. They will in turn undergo in thoughts yours;

• Keep the communication moderate and live a ways from any bad subjects. Never talk politics or faith. Don't speak about your boss, co-employee or the present day day gossip in elegant. Keep it great. This will leave you with a fantastic feeling and the man or woman you are speakme to will respect you for now not talking negatively about sincerely all and sundry else. They will take delivery of as real with you could do the same if someone attempts to speak poorly approximately them. It builds get hold of as actual with and wins you hundreds of air of mystery elements;

• Give out substantial compliments whilst relevant. It may be commenting about how a incredible deal you want a person's footwear, their new hairstyle or on a excellent task. If you be conscious a image on a person's desk, ask about it and say some aspect notable approximately the cherished character who has earned the honour to be at the character's table. Be genuine. Empty platitudes are demanding and those will fast dislike you and mistrust your intentions.

Each of these uplifting pointers is simplest going to intend a few thing in case your body language is reflecting the terms you're pronouncing.

Make effective you preserve that eye touch. Lean into the person, touch their elbow or shoulder while appropriate or shake their hand, masking the handshake with your other hand. Each of those gestures shows the character you truely care approximately them and their lives.

You do not ought to get into deep subjects. Keep it light and smooth for buddies and co-humans. It is more approximately you paying attention to them, in choice to you telling them your private problems.

You may want to make verbal exchange via the use of letting them in on little tidbits of your existence, like you are jogging on a project otherwise you're in your way to your baby's recreation. Little subjects that be a part of you to them and placed you at the same degree.

This human interaction is crucial to our personal intellectual properly-being and you may thoroughly be the handiest shining spot in another character's day. Make it take into account!

Do Your Homework eleven

This one is not going to require your pocket book. Instead, set a intention to do one or all of those uplifting pointers every day.

Start small if it makes you revel in uncomfortable. Set a purpose to take a look at the names of at the least three new people all through your ordinary day. The following week, ask each of these humans at least one direct, precise query that applies to them by myself.

This will assist you enjoy a touch better about public talking and you could start to increase your air of thriller and not using a real try. Remember that gradual and regular wins the race.

Chapter 9: Get Passionate

When you're obsessed on a topic, you will glaringly be more energetic while speaking about it. Your passion for a specific assignment, interest or cause may be palpable. People will see your ardour and will battle no longer to sense the pride. It is contagious.

When you're the leader of a enterprise business enterprise, a mission or maybe in a social setting, you want to tap into that ardour to help make your case. This is in which that self-discovery comes in. You now understand what you're clearly passionate about.

Now, it isn't going to be possible to experience that fireplace burning about the entirety, but you may find particular factors of any situation to get captivated with. This is going to require you to open up your thoughts a hint and permit your self to truly get into some factor new or possibly it's far a few aspect that has been driven to the lowest of the listing time and again...

If you need to get a assignment completed however are suffering to find out the incentive, take it domestic or take it in your place of job and take a seat down on my own with it.

Let your introvert thoughts go to artwork, digging deep into the task. You thrive on mysteries and troubles that want to be solved and, even as you permit yourself to get into it, you'll be thrilled at what you find out.

You need to be able to discover your ardour for a project, a aim or some thing it is within the front of you looking completed. Find your passion after which use your ardour to steer others. When they see you get excited and communicate with pride, it will spark their hobby.

Use your modern abilities to attract a map to the stop line or the task of completion. Sometimes, humans can't see the reason and consequently battle to get excited for something. You need to expose them the way.

This is a big benefit of an introvert. They have an innate capability to sit down down again and mull over a trouble, offer you with diverse solutions and then pick out out the pleasant one to transport in advance. Projects are completed pretty really due to the truth the charismatic introvert has frolicked thinking about the various issues that could rise up. Goals are met and the entire team can be elated.

Some strategies to help you find out your ardour are as follows.

•   Clear your mind absolutely of any preconceived mind approximately a technique, intention or a undertaking. You want to have an open mind. This is a difficult one and it's miles going to be difficult to promote to others as quickly as you have got were given found your very very own passion. Take a stroll, clear your head and switch off the negative opinion of a undertaking. Set your mind to effective and then delve in;

•	Find that one little nugget of a assignment or reason and clearly dig into it. Break the undertaking up into chunk size portions and ask your co-people to assist, with all people taking the bit that appeals to them maximum. Your venture will circulate from mundane to thrilling and passionate due to the fact all and sundry changed into allowed to do what they really cherished;

•	Think of the advantages to the assignment. Maybe you will advantage or perhaps you may be doing a little thing brilliant for others. You can be selling the paintings or supporting the ones in need. Whatever the case may be, look for the give up game. That is what you need to be obsessed with. Sometimes the art work to get there may be a warfare, however you need to preserve your eyes at the prize and keep pushing to the aspect that inspires your ardour;

•   Make a visible of the whole lot that hobbies you in life. These can be topics out of your adolescence that have been forgotten or neglected as you elderly. Take a couple of minutes to have a look at your board and look for the items/situations that sincerely make you excited. These are the elements you are virtually captivated with and could do nicely at because you like doing them;

•   Get out of the administrative center and take a walk, pass for a hike or plan a tenting experience. Get into nature and word and revel in herbal beauty. Let it fill your thoughts and refresh your soul. It is a lot much less complex to peer the beauty in things while your mind has been cleansed of the every day grind and stress this is going on the side of it;

•   Sometimes, ardour isn't going to come manifestly. In good sized, you revel in obsessed on some element for no obvious rhyme or cause. Some people are obsessed on flying and feature cherished the concept considering that they have been young youngsters. Others are afraid of it. Every character is precise and could have their non-public reviews and be interested in various things. However, a person who wasn't inquisitive about flying early on in life, also can end up in a career that dives right into that international. The extra they find out approximately flying, they greater they typically have a propensity to discover it impossible to resist. Their ardour is superior as they test extra and become an professional in a selected concern. This may be the manner you increase your very personal ardour for a selected manner or interest. Study it and you may eventually turn out to be loving it or hating it!

Do Your Homework 12

Build your creativity board. You are probable very cunning and this will be a fun project that you can delve into.

Use poster board and snap shots cut from antique magazines or draw your very personal. The concept is to make a university of things you need and experience. You can hold increasing in this as you skip. Put your creativity board somewhere you will see it often. Study it and allow your mind wander.

You will probable provide you with passion obligations a good way to take you down a road of creativity and pleasure. You can also need to carry humans on board your venture, so one can be smooth with the ardour you display for it. Your aura will show and you can discover human beings need to be part of your tasks.